Programming Environmental Improvements in Public Transportation

Programming Environmental Improvements in Public Transportation

Edmund J. Cantilli
Polytechnic Institute of New York

Lexington Books
D.C. Heath and Company
Lexington, Massachusetts
Toronto   London

Library of Congress Cataloging in Publication Data

Cantilli, Edmund J.
    Programming environmental improvements in public transportation.

    Bibliography: p.
    1. Local transit—Public opinion. 2. Local transit—Finance. I Title.
HE4281.C33   301.15'43'3884   73-11666
ISBN 0-669-87072-2

We must completely renew our cities. The alternative is disaster. Gaping needs must be met in health, in education, in job opportunities, in housing. And not a single one of these needs can be fully met until we rebuild our mass transportation systems.

Lyndon B. Johnson, 1968

Contents

List of Figures

List of Tables

Foreword

Technology in the public transportation field today is, and actually has been for some time past, at a stage where the transportation planner, designer, or engineer is capable of the physical planning, design, and construction of any public transportation system conceivable to the human mind. Adequate funding for public transportation today and for the foreseeable future, however, is seriously and regrettably lacking. Naturally, without the necessary funding, both public and private, this wealth of technology cannot be, and has not been, fully utilized.

Public transportation has changed very little over the years in terms of design, capacity for service, maintenance of facilities, and certainly in terms of meeting the desires of the public transportation patron. Lack of change in the first three areas can be attributed, possibly, to lack of funds. However, lack of progress in the fourth is most likely due to neglect, either conscious or subconscious, by the transportation planner or engineer. We may fear that we do not know enough about the patron's desires, needs, or hopes, as they relate to public transportation; or we may fear that if we *did* know them, we would have no methodology available to utilize them to assist us in allocating our limited funds for improvement of the transportation systems. We have for too long disregarded these "intangibles" and concentrated on the "tangibles" to which we are able to attach numerical values. This text, we hope, will help to change these attitudes toward the value of the opinions, desires, and needs of the riding public.

The text discusses a method of distributing funds for the improvement of public transportation facilities in which *public opinion plays an integral part* in the development of an allocation index. The book demonstrates the feasibility of combining and manipulating the "tangibles" and "intangibles" into usable numerical indexes to benefit the public. It demonstrates the usefulness of value measurement techniques, and encourages the formalizing of such techniques as important and beneficial parts of the planning process. The demonstration of concern by the transportation planner for the patrons' needs and values in planning transportation systems, as set forth in this book, will assist in bridging the communication gap between "user" and "planner." This should help in making the transportation systems more palatable to the riding public who are, in fact, those for whom the system exists.

It is appropriate that this text was written by a man who obviously has experienced the problems that are associated with trying to provide maximum transportation facilities with minimum transportation funds. He has not only heard but has listened to what the riding public has been saying concerning their needs and values, their hopes and fears. He has, more important, decided to do something about them. This text will be of benefit to the student of transportation as well as to the policy-maker. It will draw their attention to, and demonstrate the need for, the fact that, to quote the author, "The balance must be drawn between what patrons say they want, and what 'experts' say patrons need, with cost acting as an overall modifier." His demonstration of methodology to accomplish this should prove a positive step forward in the planning, construction, and maintenance of viable public transportation systems.

David W. Gwynn, P.E.
Director of Research and Development
New Jersey Department of Transportation

July 1973
Trenton, New Jersey

Preface

There is little doubt that there has been, and will continue to be, little money forthcoming from any source, public or private, or any level of government, federal, state, or local, earmarked for the specific purpose of improving the "environment" of the patron of mass-transit facilities. Studies will continue to show that the impinging factors of that environment—noise, dust, gases, light, aesthetics—can affect not only the psyche of patrons but their very physical being. Yet little attention will be paid to the improvement of such "amenities" because, the argument goes, there will never be enough money to *really* do an adequate job.

This is precisely the point addressed here: that the relatively small amounts of money that *will* be allocated for the improvement of the transit environment *can be spent effectually*. And not only effectually from the standpoint of the transit operator and his staff of "experts," but effectually from the standpoint of the *user* of the system seeing improvements which *he* would like to have made. This requires knowledge of what the user thinks and desires, of course, and from that point of view this is an area which engineers and policy-makers have steered clear of. But it is a growing necessity in urban planning and in transportation planning to provide what is desirable to the user, or plans will be blocked, and patronage will drop off. To provide what is desirable to the user, or changes in mode *desired* for reasons of amenity or *required* for reasons of environmental survival cannot be brought about except through governmental fiat.

A greater understanding, then, of our own motives and behavioral requisites, coupled with logical means of resource allocation, are the purpose of this book and the hope expressed in its pages.

Acknowledgments

Thanks are due to Professors Louis J. Pignataro, William R. McShane, and Abraham Engelberg of the Polytechnic Institute of Brooklyn, for their aid and comfort during early versions of this work. Professor Pignataro, as head of the Department of Transportation Planning and Engineering, supervised overall the project of which this study is a portion; professors McShane and Engelberg were of great help in the technical and mathematical aspects of the work. My particular thanks to Bill McShane.

Thanks also to the Urban Mass Transportation Administration of the U.S. Department of Transportation, for support of a portion of the work involved here.

Finally, much appreciation is offered to my family for their patience and forbearance, and to Mrs. Elaine Cummings for her labors in typing the manuscript.

The author accepts full responsibility for errors of fact or judgment.

Introduction

A study by the United States Department of Housing and Urban Development enumerated eight general problems, endemic to cities today, which are dependent on transportation. They are:

equality of access to urban opportunity
quality of service
congestion
efficient use of equipment and facilities
efficient use of land
urban pollution
urban development options
institutional framework and implementation[1]

This book addresses the second, quality of service, the "comfort and convenience" involved in making the choice between the personal car and public transit: the bus, subway, elevated line, or commuter suburban railroad. Public transit is too often characterized by inadequate service, crowding, noise, lack of comfort, lack of information, and danger to personal safety, among other drawbacks familiar to all. These deficiencies, besides increasing cost, have led to a loss of patronage, besides degrading the human beings, physically and psychologically, who are forced to use the systems.

Many of the urban transit systems of this country were developed as long as forty years ago, and have had limited upgrading of plant and rolling stock, stations, tunnels, and trains, since then. The capability of providing safe, comfortable, attractive, and reliable service is contingent on logically allocating limited funds to those areas which will, *in the opinion of the user of the system*, provide those features. It is the opinion of the patron, after all, that will determine the relative success of attempts to upgrade a system, an opinion based on the *user's* relative weighting of the importance of each impinging discomfort, and of its relationship to the whole transportation environment.

Since subway systems were created for the middle-income groups of their times, we should also consider the potentialities of restoring their attractivity to the middle-income groups of today, instead of watching them being forced downward to use by the poorer and poorer at higher and higher costs, while those who can, drive.

For many years the quality of urban mass transportation has been neglected and transit systems have been allowed to deteriorate. During the fifteen years from 1945 to 1960, while urban populations increased appreciably, the total number of revenue transit passengers declined from 19 billion to 8 billion passengers per year.[2] This is both a cause and a result of that deterioration.

While much current opinion advocates severe restrictions on the use of autos in urban areas, the quality of urban mass transportation systems must first be improved to the point where the systems are functionally efficient and aesthetically attractive enough to command mass acceptance. People must have transportation systems which approach the automobile in comfort and quality, and which are superior in safety and reliability, as alternatives to the auto. The auto-owning public might then be induced to voluntarily select public transportation as its major mode of transport within the urban areas.

The Housing Act of 1961 was the Federal government's formal recognition of the transportation problems of the nation's cities. It included several provisions for urban transit systems. The Act recognized the need for a national urban mass transportation program and provided financial support for much-needed experimental projects in transportation planning.

In 1964 the Urban Mass Transportation Act was introduced, and, as amended in 1966, it was designed to provide assistance by the Department of Housing and Urban Development (HUD) to state and local governments to initiate long-range programs for the development of improved transportation techniques and the planning of integrated, efficient, area-wide systems.

The Housing and Urban Development Act of 1968 set aside additional funds for urban mass transit systems, which, from July 1968, became largely the responsibility of the newly formed Department of Transportation.[3] The Urban Mass Transportation Assistance Act of 1970, which further expanded the Urban Mass Transportation Act of 1964, provided for a Federal commitment to spend at least 10 billion dollars over a twelve-year period for a program of grants and loans for financing, acquiring, constructing, and improving facilities and equipment.

The Need for Rehabilitation

Recognizing the need for rehabilitating transportation facilities which, through age and neglect, have fallen into disrepair and worse, is certainly not new. But translating such recognition into logical action is. In a study of commuter railroad stations, for instance, it was recognized that the "station is often a faded and neglected building, where travel demand is such that, except for peak hours, very few people are at the station at any one time."[4] In this manner, the station becomes an isolated and unattractive place. This does not necessarily apply in its entirety to urban mass-transit terminals, but it is certainly true that the brief exposure of individuals to a station does not usually result in a feeling of its integral importance to an entire system, or to the cityscape in general.

The awareness of the need to consider transportation termini in the context of the social fabric is again expressed by that study of suburban stations: "With the growing recognition that railroads are important to travel in an urban region, the rehabilitation of the station takes on real significance." At this point there must be a definition of the essentials contributing to a viable station: vitality, aesthetics, safety, convenience, circulation-information, and economics. As the report describes aesthetics: "The impact of the station and its surroundings on the human spirit is a real element of consideration. Regardless of its simplicity or grandeur, an attractive and well maintained [station] . . . can do much to establish an environment which promotes activity and vitality. On the other hand, design which is austere and maintenance which is non-existent appeals to few other than a passing derelict."[5]

Except for futuristic model schemes, public transportation has changed very little over the years in design and capacity for service; much less than has the private automobile. Most such systems were conceived and designed during a period when cities were poorer and more compact, and now transit naturally gives inadequate coverage and service, either to the dispersed and affluent or to the crowded poor.

Technological innovation has a great deal to offer public transit. It can provide improvements in coverage, comfort, and amenities, using modern vehicles and computer control (such as in the BART system), or it can automatically respond to individual service requests (à la Dial-A-Ride). Trains can be made smoother, quieter, and more comfortable with improved suspension, propulsion, and automatic operation; but major redesign of stations is long overdue.

It is clear, however, that the most immediate solutions to transportation problems will not be found in developing new concepts and elaborate, exclusive-right-of-way mass transportation with high speeds. More effective utilization of *existing* mass transportation systems must be developed, by improving basic services and amenities.

The importance of improving existing mass transportation systems, and designing better new ones, lies in the hope of solving overall transportation problems that are found in the imbalance between modes, the stress on individual vehicles, and the lack of attractiveness, or even capacity, of the mass modes.

So the hope is that in knowing something of the desires of people for improvement will be found the solution to how best to control modal choice. How best to utilize the natural desires of individuals for what drives them to choose the auto, with all its contingent difficulties in and around the urban areas, over other means of transportation. All this without the ultimate control: *enforced* modal choice.

The Psychology of Transportation
Mode Choice

It has been recommended all too often that an obvious solution to the nation's traffic problem is to get people out of their cars and into a mass transit system. But few have undertaken serious, scientific research to determine what kind of alternate transportation might be acceptable to users.

Engineers and urban planners have consistently overlooked or ignored the psychological needs of the individuals who are supposed to use the mass transit system which they, the engineers and planners, design.

In the view of a specialist in human behavior, the successful mass transit systems are coercive systems.[6] Commuters use them because they have no alternative. The subway system of the city of New York, for instance, is one of the most elaborate in the world, and yet "there is no more resentful group of people in the world in respect to their subways than those who use them regularly. These people take the subway for reasons of immediate speed or because they can't afford to go any other way. They don't ride the subways because they want to; they simply have no other choice. And they hate it."

One of the absolutely basic human needs, according to this authority, is the need to "locomote." When people lose control over their locomotion, they may develop various psychosomatic reactions. There is something of deep psychological importance in preserving one's freedom of movement and one's control over it. When this is limited, there is strong resentment. This explains why individuals are willing to endure a certain amount of inconvenience and inefficiency in the use of personal autos in exchange for control over their own locomotion.[7] It also suggests directions in which those of us who would attempt to attract auto drivers out of their cars might move.

Studies by the Cornell University Medical School have shown that citizens of New York are under tremendous pressures, and the levels of tension, anxiety, unhappiness, and distress are very high. *Enforced* use of mass transit is therefore undesirable from this standpoint. In boarding a train a person loses control over his immediate environment, which may produce the tensions and anxieties discovered among some urban dwellers. And yet it is apparent that a large proportion of mass transit riders are, in effect, compelled to use that mode. Since this is, and will no doubt remain, the case through necessity or future requirement, it behooves us to make that use as close to pleasurable, or acceptable, or unnoticeable, as possible.

Too little research has been done into the psychology of mass transportation. There have been some superficial demographic public-opinion surveys, but there is a great need for a good deal of basic research on what will be acceptable to people; much more than asking a few simple questions. There has to be a constant feedback on the psychology involved, and engineers and economists must remember that the absolutely rational approach is rarely the most effective way to deal with human problems.

Patron Attitude Assessment

There has been little use of attitude assessment techniques in transportation planning. As one researcher has noted, "By and large, no matter how much it thinks it knows about a given group of people through the eyes of leaders, through surveys, and physical analyses, an agency often knows very little. And yet a good deal of money is spent and many facilities are built based on very little information."[8]

The question of the citizen's *satisfaction* or *dissatisfaction* with a facility must be considered. Many have assumed that reducing patron *dissatisfaction* with a transportation facility will produce *satisfaction* with that facility. But in the field of job and personnel research one study has shown that job *satisfaction* is a function of the presence of sets of variables different from those that are present in job *dissatisfaction*, and correction of the dissatisfying elements is *not* enough to produce satisfaction.[9] No comprehensive attempts have been made to evaluate whether the same phenomenon exists in transportation and, if it should be true, what elements are "satisfiers" and what elements are "dissatisfiers." Money is spent on improving dissatisfiers with very little thought to the satisfiers. The proper use of attitude surveys should be to obtain indications of potential *satisfiers*.

One of the most critical elements of attitude surveys is *sampling*. A sampling procedure is considered to be accurate if it is *unbiased*, meaning that the sample is not overloaded with one kind of person. The *precision* of the sample is determined directly by the number of persons sampled, and the lack of bias in the questions asked.

Random sampling is used to eliminate systematic bias. It is also a means of assuring oneself that the sample is representative of the general population, and that the findings may be said to be applicable to the general population.

Since transportation is a subsystem of a community, which is composed of people, important improvements can be made in social situations through the improvement of transportation. More information is needed about people, however, their attitudes, values, and socioeconomic situations. Attitude studies can be used to help planners in developing and evaluating alternatives, and in dealing effectively with citizens. They can help transportation planners to be more responsive to the community. Making attitude surveys an integral element in the transportation planning process will help in dealing with community values.

Resource Allocation

Current methods of allocating funds for the maintenance and improvement of public transportation facilities have usually evolved in an unscientific manner. Such methods as there are can generally be called political: typically, a highly placed member of the operating agency makes it known that he is dissatisfied with the quality of a given attribute of the system. This aspect then becomes the object of feverish activity on the part of numerous lower-echelon officials and workers who eventually develop a program to alleviate the condition. Or, the operating agency must respond to the critical comments of a mayor, governor, or other public figure, who in turn has been stimulated by public discontent, as manifested by newspaper articles, or complaints of citizens' groups.

Disregarding routine maintenance schedules and inspections which lead to the replacement of light bulbs, deteriorating structural members, and handrails, it is fair to say that a scientific approach has rarely been used, with the result that the *opinion* and *desires* and *needs* of the riding public, for whom the system was, after all, designed, have been sadly neglected.

This book discusses a means of distributing funds for the improvement of mass transportation facilities in which public opinion plays an integral role in the development of an allocation index. In addition, the following factors have been taken into account:

1. The need to quantify the "intangibles" of everyday amenities;
2. The necessity of relating improvement to meaningful degrees of change; and
3. The existence of cost-utility methodology.

The last consideration has been of greatest importance to those who have found it difficult to allocate funds for the improvement of "amenities," or intangibles, in transportation facilities. The problem of resource allocation is, in fact, generally made more difficult when relating cost-benefit techniques to the intangibles of benefit, or disbenefit, to some consumer of services. In relation specifically to transportation facilities, it comes down to those intangible aspects of the transportation service provided, beyond the basic and time-related aspects of people-movement, which can be called "qualities" of the system. These are usually translated into a scale of values which can be summarized into levels of "good," "bad," or "indifferent," with attempts at intermediate levels of subjective rating.

But cost-benefit analysis requires translation of this kind of subjective evaluation into quantitative values, which must eventually be capable of a relationship with monetary values for ultimately comparing them to costs. This is a major problem area.

In this book previous attempts at solving this problem were considered, and a methodology has been developed that will potentially bring the patron's desires to bear in some way in the apportionment of funds for the planning, construction, or maintenance and improvement of public modes of transportation. This participation of the *user* in decisions concerning his health, safety, and well-being while using a transportation facility is one of the novel aspects of this study.

The transportation community has been criticized for a lack of concern for community values. It must be demonstrated clearly that value measurement techniques are sound and useful. In addition, a general reluctance to formalizing such techniques as an accepted part of the planning process must be dropped, and a new enthusiasm developed in its place, for finding out exactly what it is people want, whether they express it or not.[10]

Part I
"Community Values" and Environmental "Amenities"

1

Allocation Techniques and "Community Values"

A Justification for This Approach

If we accept the view that "quality of life," a heretofore rarely considered factor, must be considered in planning and operating cities, then human behavior must be taken into account to ensure that needed facilities and services will actually be useful once implemented, and that they will accomplish the purpose and produce the effects for which they were designed.[1]

The desirability of taking social criteria into consideration in planning and implementing any kind of project is self-evident. And yet economists can say, "There is . . . good reason to ignore so-called 'non-market benefits.' . . . The aesthetic and humanitarian contributions of transportation expenditures seem small, and it is difficult to find clearly defined groups of worthy individuals that are either seriously harmed or greatly benefited by these expenditures."[2]

In the past, transportation planners and engineers emphasized efficiency of movement in selecting criteria for planning and designing facilities. Measurement of costs and benefits, with some emphasis on the viewpoints of the users and the financing agencies, has played a part in program and project evaluation, and will no doubt continue to do so. But it has become clear that factors related to other community values must also be considered in planning and designing transportation facilities.[3]

And yet, in spite of this apparently recognized need for attention to community values, little support has been given to efforts to consider these values in quantitative terms. In spite of several research projects on measuring and comparing the perceptions and needs of the public, many planners still find it difficult to use value measurement. A possible reason is that the measurement of such individual and group values is based on assumptions and techniques that originated in the social sciences, and are very different from the methods learned by engineers and physical scientists. In addition, the social sciences can be considered poorly developed in comparison with the older natural sciences. Measures, concepts, and theoretical structures have not been agreed upon and the problems are very complex. Therefore only limited attention has been given to this problem.[4]

Transportation planners have often underestimated the capabilities of value measurement techniques and overestimated their limitations. A difficulty in quantifying human responses to elements of the physical environment is the subjectivity of the investigator's involvement.

3

The literature concerning the application of cost-effectiveness analysis to social values is quite meager. While many scholars and urban planners have arrived at systematic means of evaluating social considerations, few have extended these techniques to the point of basing financial decisions on their results. A study of benefit-cost analysis in the area of transportation (as concerns social values) led to the conclusion that "no definitive, explicitly formulated set of criteria now exist by which capital projects on transportation can be judged."[5] Nor were there any "analytic methods which were comprehensive, theoretically justifiable, operational or significant." In fact, "there is a 'shocking gap' in the literature when one looks for guidance in studying the economics and social factors in urban transportation."

In attacking and solving the problems now facing the modern urban transportation planner with ever-increasing frequency, it is therefore absolutely necessary that either entirely new methods be developed, or that existing limited techniques be combined and synthesized into new tools which are more comprehensive and more powerful than current methods. A look at available tools is therefore necessary.

Concepts Available

Measures of Effectiveness

From a review of current methodology, it appears that the first task in developing a measure of effectiveness is to provide a way to transform efficiencies relative to different objectives into a common measure.[6] This requires a method of "weighting" the units in terms of which the objectives are expressed. The relative values of these units must be determined. This relative value is the *weight* of the unit of the corresponding objective.

The second problem is to develop a way of expressing efficiency. This involves the construction of an *efficiency function.* By combining the weights and efficiency functions we can obtain an *effectiveness function.*

This is accomplished here by learning the relative distance from an ideal (comfort) level of existing conditions in a station or terminal.

In this case the "efficiency of a course of action" can be interpreted as the best choice based upon various considerations: patron desire, cost, and relative importance (due to current condition).

Utility Theory

This approach shows an interest in people's preferences or values, with assumptions about a person's preferences that enable them to be represented in numerically useful ways.[7] The *predictive* approach,[8] the attempt to discern what people *will do* under a given set of circumstances, appears to be more applicable to the present situation. In this context, it may be considered to be based on a study of the basic psychology of the human being, with emphasis on predicting his satisfaction with, and reaction to, a given variable. But while utility theory has been used in brand preference, the food industry, corporate strategies, evaluation of product defects, and other pursuits, it has not been applied so far in transportation cost allocation, except as far as it is supposed to be the "common sense of decision-making."

From its origins in economics, utility theory can be considered to represent the choices of a "rational man" making his decisions. But psychologists, and transportation agencies, are interested in describing or predicting *actual choice behavior*, whether or not it is "rational." At the present time the predictive work carried out by psychologists offers little help to the decision-maker. Most of the theories tested are not good predictors of choice behavior. Most practical situations are different from experimental ones because they are more complex and nonrepetitive.

Value Measurement

Four approaches to value measurement relative to the transportation field have been suggested:

1. *Observe* individual behavior respecting *existing* transportation systems, and from such behavior derive a description of the system which is relevant to the individual, and derive the relative importance of each dimension to him.

2. *Observe* individual behavior in a *simulated* transportation system, using mechanical devices or games, and infer from the results a description of the system and the relative importance of each dimension to the individual.

3. *Measure* patron opinion and preference concerning the *existing* transportation system, and develop a description of the system as seen by the individual, and the relative importance of each dimension to him.

4. *Measure* opinions and preferences concerning a *hypothetical* transportation system, and develop a description of the system and the relative importance of each dimension of the system to the individual.

Even when the immediate satisfaction of patron desires is not possible, the knowledge gained from such studies will permit planners to anticipate community reaction more accurately, and help them to prepare a more effective public relations effort.[9]

Related Studies

Similar techniques have been used for some time in the political sphere, where there is the use of public opinion polls by politicians, with the results being used to develop a course of action in response to the apparent desires of the people.

In resource allocation, a pioneer in the use of this technique for improving service to the people is the Bell Telephone Laboratories. Experiments were conducted to improve the quality of telephone service by asking large numbers of users to rate the quality of various features of the service as "Good," "Fair," or "Bad."[10] Controlled experiments were conducted in which a selected group of people would engage in a telephone conversation, and a larger group (of about one hundred persons, not randomly selected) would monitor the conversation from listening stations especially constructed for that purpose. Each listener would then fill out a questionnaire rating features such as cross-talk, voice volume, disturbances due to static, and echo, as "Good," "Fair," or "Bad." The results were then analyzed in a manner which provided information concerning consumer dissatisfaction with the various features of the telephone service. These results were, in turn, used by management to allocate resources for improving the telephone service in proportion to the dissatisfaction expressed with the various features of the service.

More recently, Abt Associates conducted a study in which they used, as their vehicle of data collection, a technique suggested by Churchman and Ackoff.[11] The technique was used primarily to develop a ranking of personal preferences on various aspects of urban mass transit systems. Although this study was not intended to relate to resource allocation, some of its results were similar to those achieved by Bell in its experiments on quality of telephone service, and could have been used as a guide to resource allocation if it had been so desired.

Another similarity between the studies conducted by Bell and Abt is that the people answering the questionnaires were not drawn from a random sampling, but were specifically selected groups. It is quite probable that such procedures create biases in answers. Surveying users randomly eliminates such biases, and allows the development of preference rankings which are more truly indicative of the desires of all patrons of a system.

One finding is that the attitudes of many of the persons responding to questions concerning transportation facilities are independent of demographic and census characteristics.[12] This implies that patrons' attitudes cannot be predicted from common census data on age, income, education, and family size, making it difficult to use analytical tools such as regression analysis; this could explain the fact that there has been little variance in typical attitude prediction studies. The majority of the respondents in such studies as have been made favor improvements in public mass transit, particularly in urban areas where it is recognized as a vital part of metropolitan life, even though, or perhaps as a reflection of the fact that, attitudes toward mass transit are generally negative (in comparison to attitudes toward the automobile).[13]

Analytical Technique

A generalized method is presented by Jessiman:

1. Itemize the objectives.
2. Select the parameter which is the best measure of each objective.
3. Assign a weight or utility value to each of the objectives.
4. For each objective, examine the parameter chosen as the measure of that objective, and determine, using a scale such as a utility curve, the value for that alternative.
5. For each alternative, sum up the values assigned for all objectives to arrive at the alternative with the highest total value; i.e., the one which best satisfies the complete set of objectives.[14]

Cost-Effectiveness

Perhaps the closest in concept to the methodology developed in this book is a cost-effectiveness study of urban transportation,[15] in which comparisons were made of existing systems in various cities, and of various present and future modes, and of their costs and benefits. A division was made between social costs and benefits capable of *quantitative* description, and those amenable only to *qualitative* description. Besides measures of service, such as travel times and accidents, there were measures of "amenity" (pollution and physical discomfort).

An attempt was made to identify the population groups upon which costs and benefits are "incident," or to whom they pertain. Summaries of cost-benefit measures are presented, in that study, in monetary and physical units.

Surrogate measures of "inconvenience" were:

> congestion time
> "excess" time (waiting, transferring)
> exertion (walking and driving)
> "index of privacy" (vehicles/traveler)

The user cost-benefits considered were:

> reliability
> stress
> noise
> comfort and convenience
> pleasure
> aesthetics
> choice
> privacy

These were assigned grades by "experts" on a qualitative scale from A to D, with + or − qualifications. The "experts" were staff personnel who had participated in the detailed city studies. They were polled concerning the relative ranking. These judges were surveyed to find out what subjective grades might be assigned by various segments of the public.[16]

Cost-Utility

In evaluating candidate traffic signal systems, a study used a similar "expert" ranking system.[17] For benefits that could not be explicitly measured in dollars, a proxy value was developed to measure system benefit, or "utility."

By combining cost estimates for the candidate systems with a developed utility measure, a cost-utility analysis was performed approximating the cost-benefit technique. The Churchman, Ackoff, and Arnoff technique for determining relative values of system goals,[18] a technique which measures utility of preference, was used with "intangibles" as well as tangibles. Since weighting can be accomplished by either individuals or a group, this study included evaluations by professional staff members.

The weighting was done by providing the selected group with a set of randomly-ordered goal definitions. Goals were then ranked in importance, and values were assigned to the rankings.

Broad categories were first weighted, then further subcategories within each "goal" were also weight-rated. The final set of qualitative evaluations measured the degree to which each candidate system satisfied a given utility measure. The internal scale value (j) was multiplied by the weight of the utility measure (w), to develop a utility statement (jw), for each candidate. The total utility value Σjw) then represents how well a given candidate satisfies the goal under consideration.

Σjw is then multiplied by the goal weight (W_i).

$\Sigma jw \times (W_i)$ = the weighted utility value (G_i) for each candidate.

After all values G_i have been determined, they can be combined into a single utility or "effectiveness" measure for each system.[19]

Cost-Benefit

This kind of analysis requires consideration of many factors in terms of their costs and benefits. They include monetary measures of investment and operating costs, and the more intangible considerations referred to as "social" costs and benefits, discussed previously.

One investigator suggests that the process of comprehensive evaluation can be divided into four main categories:

1. Dollar costs of investment and operation.
2. User benefits and costs (other than dollar outlays).
3. Social costs and benefits, capable of quantitative description.
4. Social costs and benefits which are amenable only to qualitative descriptions and analyses.[20]

He finds that if all measures cannot be reduced to a single evaluative standard, the final product must be a "ledger" of separate entries. But this appears to be begging the question, which *demands* conversion of the "intangibles" into numerical factors. In this book *all* factors, both tangible and intangible, are reduced to monetary amounts by the simple process of having the patron, himself, rate the need for improvement of those amenities in monetary terms.

One study tackled the larger meaning of "cost" and "benefit," as presented here, by assuming that each individual (or group) has a set of preferences concerning the effects of transportation on his situation. Whatever effects he feels positively about may be considered benefits, whether they include an inflow of dollars, stopping an outflow of money, more comfort, time saved, or beauty observed. That is, a *benefit* depends on the *recipient's evaluation of the situation*, and not on that of an objective observer. Costs are defined in the same subjective manner, in terms of *liabilities*. By this interpretation, no phenomenon is purely a benefit, or only a cost.

What *people* consider beneficial is the question. A list of social or personal values about which there is little disagreement in our society could be developed without much difficulty. Whether they are absolutely good or bad is not the major concern. Nor does the majority of the people have to adopt them wholeheartedly. It is only necessary to know that some people care about these issues enough to be pleased or displeased with transportation systems affecting those values.[21]

The table of criteria of transportation costs and benefits in that study included the following, among others:

pollution
traffic accidents
noise
stress
disease
convenience
comfort
privacy
pleasure

aesthetics
prestige
sociological integration
political power

Some Specific Tools

Linear Programming

A linear programming formulation of this problem would start with identification of x_i, the amount of improvement of factor i (number of units of improvement), c_i, the "utility" or improving factor i one unit (this would be a measure of the "satisfaction" provided patrons by this one unit), and a_i, the cost of improving factor i one unit.

In linear programming, c_i and a_i must be *linear*, i.e., adding one unit of factor i produces c_i units of "satisfaction" at a_i units of cost. In the present case, however, each improvement level varies in both *cost* and *utility*.

If each unit of improvement were *defined* as bringing about a *constant* amount of utility (c_i) it could be said that $c_i x_i$ is linear, since x_i units of improvement would bring about $c_i x_i$ units of utility. However, *costs* would not be uniform.

To *approximate* linearity, define each unit of i as producing constant c_i units of "satisfaction," and an *average* cost a_i, so that all variables are equal for each unit of improvement. At this point additional constraints must be developed; each x_i will have an upper limit:

$$x_i \leqslant b_i \tag{1.1}$$

and a lower limit:

$$x_i \geqslant d_i \tag{1.2}$$

It is apparent that while linear programming could conveniently be applied, the many compromises which would have to be accepted would make its ultimate applicability to real-life situations of doubtful value.

Dynamic Programming

Consider a simple problem involving three amenities, each exhibiting three steps to comfort, with incremental costs and utility values as shown in Table 1-1.

A graphical display of potential route-choices would then show the complexity of the process (Figure 1-1).

Table 1-1
Dynamic Programming–An Example

| | Amenity | | | | | |
| | 3 | | 2 | | 1 | |
Level	Cost to Reach	Utility Value	Cost to Reach	Utility Value	Cost to Reach	Utility Value
3	1800	4	800	1	1800	2
2	1400	2	400	1	1000	1
1	800	1	400	2	800	1

In such a case, following Hadley, the number of comparisons to be made would be:

$$C = b \left[n + \frac{(n-1)(b+1)}{2} \right] + n \tag{1.3}$$

where n = the number of variables (three amenities in this case) and b = the number of subdivisions to be checked (thirty-four from Figure 1-1):

$$C = 34 \left[3 + \frac{(2)(35)}{2} \right] + 3 = 34(38) + 3 = 1295 \text{ calculations.}[22]$$

It is apparent, then, that a real-life example such as the one to be used in this study, with 11 variables (amenities), and 441,000,000 subdivisions to be checked, will develop an enormous number of calculations. Hadley noted that dynamic programming may study one-tenth of the possible subdivisions to be checked; if *one-one hundredth* of the subdivisions, or 4,410,000 were checked, the number of calculations (Equation 1.3) would be:

$$C = 4,410,000 \left[11 + \frac{(10)(4,410,000)}{2} \right] + 11$$

$$= 4.41 \times 10^6 \, (22.05 \times 10^6) + 11$$

$$= 97.24 \times 10^{12}$$

Even modern, high-speed computers would require inordinate amounts of time for such calculations.

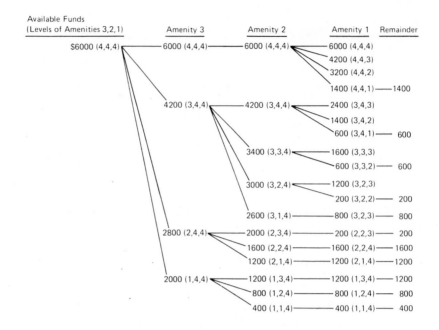

Figure 1-1. Dynamic Programming Route Choices

2

Assessing "Community Values"

Patron Opinion

It is difficult to find surveys similar in intent to the purposes of this book. Most of those which exist are evaluations of modal choice.

Surveys which might be considered as related to the present approach have generally been designed to describe the transportation attitudes and behavior of specific segments of the population. Either they are general questionnaires concerning other urban and environmental concerns, including transportation, or they are attempts at determining why modal choices are made, and what would be needed to change such choices. At any rate, they give insights into the public's problems with mass transportation, generally if not specifically.

The majority of the respondents in those studies which exist favor improvements in public mass transit, particularly in urban areas where it is recognized as a vital component of metropolitan life. This is true in spite of, or as a reflection of, the fact that attitudes toward mass transit are generally negative (in comparison to the automobile).[1] Generally speaking, as regards the purposes of this study, the actual comfort provided by the transit vehicle, and, presumably, the transit station, can be very important in contributing to commuter satisfaction.[2]

Some Pertinent Studies

For a general view of transportation attitudes and behavior, the NCHRP reports dealing with this subject are the best source.[3] These reports from a national study have shown that there is close ego involvement with the automobile as a way of life in the United States. Most respondents in the study felt that improvements should be made in both automobile and public transportation. In metropolitan areas, public transportation was recognized as a vital part of our way of life, and worthy of continued and accelerated emphasis. But attitudes toward *present* public transportation services and facilities tended to be generally negative rather than positive.

While the automobile was favored most as a mode of transportation, it was not favored at the expense of public transportation. The individual who rated the automobile high as a mode of transportation did not necessarily rate public transportation low; and the person who was dissatisfied with the transportation

13

attributes of public transportation was not necessarily satisfied with the attributes of the automobile. For instance, 46 percent of respondents felt that more money should be spent on public transportation. Those favoring greater expenditures for public transportation were more likely to live in the East or West, in metropolitan areas.

The following more specific studies reveal other aspects of public attitude:

1. One survey of 350 households in Baltimore covered about 550 individuals sixteen years of age or older.[4] The research objectives were to determine the attributes of an "ideal" transportation system, quantify the relative importance of each attribute, and evaluate existing transportation systems with respect to these ideal characteristics. What emerged as the most important factor was system *reliability*, the ability to arrive at one's destination safely, on schedule, without mechanical failure (see Table 2-1).

The pertinent questions asked in that interview survey included:

- What attributes do consumers regard as salient in typical recent trips?
- What is the relative importance of the attributes of each trip purpose?
- What is the perceived relative importance of the attributes for all trip purposes (i.e., of an overall, ideal system)?
- To what extent, and how, are demographics and specific trip characteristics of respondents related to perceived importance of trip mode attributes?

A summary of the importance of factors within each trip purpose by rank is seen in Table 2-2.

Table 2-1

Transportation Factors Ranked in Order of Importance in Baltimore Study

Rank	Factor
1	Reliability of achieving destination
2	Convenience and comfort
3	Travel time
4	Cost
5	Independence of control (e.g., vehicle, route, schedule)
6	Traffic and congestion
7	Social (e.g., travel companions)
8	Age of vehicle
9	Diversions (e.g., scenery)

Source: G.A. Brunner, et al., "User Determined Attributes of Ideal Transportation Systems: An Empirical Study," University of Maryland, College Park, Maryland, June 1966 (PB 173730).

Table 2-2
Importance of Factors within Each Trip Purpose: Baltimore Study

Factors	Work-School	Shopping-Personal Business	In-town Social	Out-of-town Social
Repairs	1	1	1	1
Reliability	2	–	–	–
Speed	3	4	6	5
Cost	4	3	4	4
Independence	5	5	5	6
Traffic	6	7	7	8
Age of vehicle	7	8	8	7
Family & friends	8	6	3	2
Diversion	–	9	9	9
Comfort	–	2	2	–
Avoid annoyances	–	–	–	3

Source: V. Salmon, "Noise in Mass-Transit Systems," in Stanford Research Institute Journal, No. 16, Sept. 1967.

The rating method was based on a system of number assignment, thus:

of no importance	=	1
of little importance	=	2
some importance	=	3
important	=	4
very important	=	5

2. Some other studies have considered similar variables, including:

frequency of service	challenge
having to change vehicles	safety
flow of traffic	urgency
speed	status
convenience	packaging
expense	need to own an automobile
comfort	availability of public transportation
distance	flexibility
crowdedness	weather
tension; fatigue	operating cost
sense of freedom	traffic and congestion
scenery	ease of driving
travel time	stop signs[a]

3. Sommers and Leimkuhler describe a questionnaire survey of midwestern businessmen designed to disclose the reasons for choosing airline or automobile travel for business trips 112 miles and 274 miles in length (see Table 2-3).[6] In that study, noise is ranked at the bottom of the importance scale. The authors draw the hasty conclusion from this that "The airport designer need not be overly concerned with noise. Current levels are acceptable to passengers." The fact that these are businessmen traveling in a state of luxury appears not to have been considered.

4. In studies in Baltimore and Philadelphia attempting to relate transportation choice to the consumer's viewpoint, the order of importance of various factors came forth as shown in Table 2-4.[7]

Some other conclusions of these studies are:

    a. Those who used automobiles reported more satisfaction with the auto than those who used public transportation.

    b. Those who used public transportation reported more satisfaction with public transportation than did those who took the automobile.

    c. Public transportation riders reported slightly more satisfaction with public transportation than auto riders did with the auto.

According to this source, eight factors are of greatest importance for most consumers in making transportation decisions. The order of importance is:

1. reliability of destination achievement
2. convenience and comfort
3. traveling time
4. cost
5. condition of the vehicle
6. self-esteem and autonomy
7. traffic and congestion
8. diversions

Table 2-3
Business Travel Factor Importance Rankings

Rank	Factor
1	Total door-to-door travel time
2	Convenience
3	Safety
4	Weather reliability
5	Comfort
6	Cost
7	Travel noise

Source: A.M. Sommers and F.F. Leimkuhler, "A Nondemographic Factor V/STOL Prediction Model," in *ORSA Bulletin*, Vol. 16, Supplement 2, Fall 1968.

Table 2-4
Trip Purpose and Consumer Opinion

Work Trip		Nonwork Trip	
Baltimore	*Philadelphia*	*Baltimore*	*Philadelphia*
1. Repairs	1. Reliability	1. Repairs	1. Reliability
2. Reliability	2. Travel	2. Comfort	2. Weather
3. Speed	3. Weather	3. Cost	3. Convenience
4. Cost	4. Cost	4. Speed	4. Cost
5. Independence	5. State of vehicle	5. Independence	5. Travel time
6. Traffic	6. Unfamiliarity	6. Family & friends	6. State of vehicle
7. Age of vehicle	7. Self-esteem	7. Traffic	7. Congestion
8. Family & friends	8. Diversions	8. Age of vehicle	8. Unfamiliarity
			9. Diversions
			10. Self-esteem

Source: S.J. Hille, et al., *Studying Transportation Systems from the Consumer Viewpoint: Some Recommendations*, Maryland University, September 1967 (PB 176484).

5. Reduction or abolition of fares is suggested from time to time as a cure-all. But in considering this as a possibility, a study to determine how many patrons would transfer to public transportation if fares were reduced found that, while there would be an appreciable increase, "even greater numbers would transfer given improvements in the speed and comfort of public transport."[8] Over a third of the motorists in a study of more than four hundred regular commuters said that they would transfer if some or all of the improvements were made. Of the total sample, for instance, 39 percent said they would use public transportation if it were *quicker than it is now*; 35 percent would use it if it were *more frequent than it is now*; and 42 percent if it were *more comfortable than it is now*. On the other hand, of motorists who said they would *not* use free public transportation, 23 percent gave *convenience* as a reason; 21 percent gave *speed*; and 24 percent said *comfort* was the problem.

6. In a home-interview survey, conducted in 1964, of seven hundred persons, questions were grouped under convenience, comfort, and cost.[9] The attitude responses were found to be apparently independent of the socioeconomic characteristics of the household, its location, or travel demands. The responses to the attitude questions did not provide any reasons for the choice of either mode of transportation, other than the subjective preferences of the user, where trip purpose permitted the choice (see Tables 2-5, 2-6, and 2-7).

The transportation system attributes for which the car was most heavily favored are:

more convenience in scheduling trips
more independence in selecting destinations

less time-consuming
more privacy
less walking involved
more comfortable

Table 2-5

Attitude Responses by Transit Riders about Transit Mode

Transportation System Attribute	Proportion of Responses Favoring Transit
Less total cost	84%
Safe	75
Provides period of relaxation	70
Less tiring	65
Less frustrating	61
Warmer in winter	52
More reliable	43
Less time-consuming	34

Source: R.W. Smith, *A Pilot Study of Relationships Between Socio-Economic Factors, User Attitudes and Preferences and Urban Transportation System Attributes*, Damas and Smith Ltd., Toronto, Canada, April 1969.

Table 2-6

Transportation System Attributes Rated by Both Car Driver and Transit Rider in Favor of Car Mode

1. More privacy
2. More comfortable
3. Cleaner
4. More prestige
5. Provides period of relaxation

Source: S.J. Hille, et al., *Studying Transportation Systems from the Consumer Viewpoint: Some Recommendations*, Maryland University, September 1967.

7. Another study considered the question of whether modal choice is made because of external or internal environments. In this study the train or bus was considered to have the greatest advantages in comfort and convenience and safety over the private car or subway/city bus (see Tables 2-8 and 2-9).[10]

Reasons given for choice of travel mode, were in the following order: time; cost; comfort. (Two thirds of the trips were by auto.) Not having a seat, and the necessity of making a transfer, had a significant influence on choice of transportation.

8. Major problem areas found in another study were:

a. There is less than adequate, or confusing, communication between carriers, or the terminal authority, and the public; and

b. There is a failure to apply available technology to problems of

- Terminal design (such as intermode convenience)
- Information (such as displays, and answers to inquiries)
- Baggage handling

Table 2-7
Ranking of Attitude Response by Degree of Concern

Transportation System Attribute	Proportion of "No Concern" and "Undecided" Responses
More convenient in scheduling trips	3%
Less time-consuming	3
Less walking involved	5
More independence in selecting destinations	6
More comfortable	6
More privacy	11
Less tiring	13
Warmer in winter	13
Not so hot in summer	15
Less frustrating	16
More reliable	16
Provides a period of relaxation	20
Less total cost	20
Cleaner	24
Safer	25
More prestige	52

Source: S.J. Hille, et al., *Studying Transportation Systems from the Consumer Viewpoint: Some Recommendations*, Maryland University, September 1967.

9. Project DATA, in Philadelphia, was interested in "user perceptions" of relevant socioeconomic, downtown-related, planning parameters.[11] They found that quantification of these variables "is not an easy task." Their experience showed that users attach different levels of importance to the variables, depending on the trip purpose (e.g., *trip time* may be very important for an essential trip, such as a work trip, while *comfort* may be the most important for a pleasure trip—a nonessential trip). Furthermore, for the same type of trip, different types of people attach different levels of importance to the variables, a conclusion inconsistent with some other studies.

Unfortunately, the determination of users' perceptions of what the study calls "downtown place" are even more nebulous than the user-transportation-

Table 2-8
Rankings by Various Groups: Subway, City Bus

Ranking by	
Clerks	1. Comfort and convenience
	2. Round-trip cost
	3. Total travel time
	4. Walking and transferring time
	5. Safety
Professionals	1. Comfort and convenience
	2. Total travel time
	3. Safety
	4. Round-trip cost
	5. Walking and transferring time
Administrators	1. Comfort and convenience
	2. Total travel time
	3. Safety
Executives	1. Comfort and convenience
	2. Round-trip cost
	3. Total travel time

system interaction. The report concluded that these perceptions have many psychological overtones, and have to be attacked at that level. "One cannot ask cogent questions about comfort when it cannot even be defined."

The following "link variables" were defined for Project DATA:

a. Physical comfort: includes considerations of energy expenditure and weather influence. The term *physical comfort* is defined as including those factors which have direct relationships with, or bearing upon, the five senses.

b. Mental comfort: includes considerations of perceived security, privacy, cleanliness, and diversions. Mental comfort includes those perceptual qualities or feelings which are related to the ease of the human mind in relation to its bodily comfort (see Table 2-10).

Each variable component was assigned a number (from 0 to 10) for each mode, which reflected the project staff's judgment as to the relative cost of each component with respect to each mode. The values for components comprising one variable (e.g., *energy expenditure* and *weather influence* are components of physical discomfort) were added together to obtain a composite variable value. This was an arbitrary decision, but "any other decision would have been at least as arbitrary."

In Table 2-11 the values for the physical discomfort index may be interpreted to mean that the cost associated with the walking mode is four times as great as

Table 2-9
Rankings by Various Groups: Subway and Bus

Ranking by	
Clerks	1. Seat and elbow room and possible to read and write on the way
	2. Low tension and effort
	3. Low noise and vibration
Professionals	1. Seat and elbow room
	2. Low noise and vibration
	3. Low tension and effort
	4. Seat and elbow room and possible to read and write on the way
Administrators	1. Seat and elbow room
	2. Low tension and effort
	3. Seat and elbow room and possible to read and write on the way
Executives	1. Seat and elbow room
	2. Low noise and vibration
	3. Low tension and effort
	4. Seat and elbow room and possible to read and write on the way

that associated with the bus mode, and nearly seven times as great as that associated with the auto and taxi modes.

In general, the results of these studies underscore the importance of *safety, reliability*, and *time-cost savings* in attempting to attract drivers to public transportation. But in addition, the extreme importance given to *convenience* and *comfort* in study after study illustrates the need for returning aging public transit systems to some competitive level of attractivity. In sum, it is quite apparent from these results that public transportation will be used by consumers if it meets their needs.

The users of transportation systems, then, and other affected citizens, are coming to be viewed as key elements in system design, evaluation, and operation. Sommers finds citizen surveys to be a necessary step in generating valid data. A "crucial factor," he says, "in the solution of urban and intercity transportation problems is the citizen traveler, the buyer and user of transportation services."[12] The patron's demand for a voice in the design, planning, and operation of transportation services and innovations may take the form of political action, but it may also appear in the form of demonstrations and even

Table 2-10

Characteristics of Transportation and Implications: Project DATA

User-oriented Characteristics	System Implications
Education (information)	Placing of information, graphic design
Lighting	Lighting design
Comfort	Human factors design
Weather protection	Station and access point design, pathway design

Source: Final Report, *Project DATA*, Vol. 3, Appendixes, Case Western Reserve University, et al., Cleveland, Ohio, May 1969.

Table 2-11

Discomfort Indexes: Project DATA

Mode	Values for Link Cost Variables	
	Physical Discomfort Index	Mental Discomfort Index
Auto	3	4
Bus	5	27
Taxi	3	16
Walk	20	23

Source: W. Lassow, E.L. Lustenader, and K. Schoch, *A Thermal Model for the Evaluation of Subway Ventilation and Air Conditioning*, ASCE-ASME National Transportation Engineering Meeting, Seattle, Washington, July 26-30, 1971.

sabotage and violence, as it has recently in Japan. There are few ways in which the citizen can influence formal transportation planning processes, and yet he must still finally use and pay for the end product. Citizen satisfaction is now a necessary consideration in facility design. It must now be a major consideration in facility *improvement*.

Questionnaire Surveys

Questionnaire surveys are more and more popular in planning circles, and can also be considered democratically desirable as a means of determining user and nonuser attitudes. To be effective, however, such surveys must concentrate on *current* transportation problems, and not on future or proposed systems. The user forms an opinion about the system he rides every day. The analyst must remember this if he wants to get estimates of real attitudes and behavior.[13] Some attempts at obtaining reactions to proposed future systems have generally produced enthusiasm, indifference, or hostility. This tells little about what the attitudes and behavior of riders will be when the facility is actually operating. It is apparently better to measure reactions toward *existing* systems, decide on the reasons for these reactions, and then attempt to predict the acceptance of future transportation innovations.[14]

While panels of "experts" have been used effectively, it is apparent that genuine information on citizen opinion can only be obtained by communicating with the citizens themselves.[15] Interview surveys are effective ways of obtaining this information. In many areas of life questionnaire surveys probably do not actually uncover user attitudes, needs, preferences, and behavior because of social taboos or inhibitions. But it is believed that transportation, as a problem which all people confront to some degree, does not produce such restrictions on critical comment perhaps because it is not highly personal. Questionnaire surveys on current transportation problems have produced valid representations of actual attitudes, preferences, needs, and behavior.

3 Some Human Environmental Factors

There appears to have been no comprehensive research conducted to isolate the components which affect passenger comfort and to rank these components in order of importance. And yet there are studies which show that when the major inconveniences of mass transit are reduced, passenger volumes increase.[1]

This chapter explores a number of human environmental qualities which might be chosen as the "amenities" to be rated by a given riding public, for the purpose of developing incremental levels noticeable to the average patron.

The term "passenger comfort" is confusing to many transportation researchers. Since the components of comfort are rarely defined in attitude surveys, a definite rank order cannot be ascertained, but there is some evidence that comfort factors are not as important as safety, reliability, and time.

Most writers refer only to low-frequency vibration and other oscillatory motions under the category of comfort; often this aspect is vaguely called "ride quality." Sometimes this definition is extended to include noise and lateral (outward) nonoscillatory forces on passengers.

Other researchers think of comfort only in terms of seating space and ventilation. According to Sheehan, the critical dimensions and factors affecting passenger comfort in transit vehicles are headroom; seat width and design; aisle width and seating arrangements; door location; width and height; lighting; and such factors as noise, vibration, and acceleration.[2]

The "amenities" chosen for discussion in this book are the following factors related to rapid transit (rail) facilities:

escalators
cleaner stations
station redecoration
station heating in winter
quieter stations
better station lighting
station air conditioning
better train service
more police in stations
improved washroom facilities

The areas considered in this study, which embrace the above categories, are:

convenience (escalators, train service, washrooms)
aesthetics (decor; redecoration)
temperature (heating, air conditioning)
noise
illumination (lighting)
safety (police)

The choices might just as easily have concerned buses, and might then have included such factors as bus stop location, comfort, need for protection from weather, acceleration-deceleration, etc. Or the entire point of view might be taken to be that of the *nonpatron* who is affected by the transportation system, and the factors would then include:

noise
odor
annoyance
air pollution

But returning to passenger comfort criteria, the subject may be roughly divided into three tolerance levels:

1. An upper physiological limit, beyond which the condition is physically intolerable;
2. A limit, beyond which the body will survive, but will be uncomfortable or unsatisfied; and
3. A psychological condition in which one's body is "comfortable" but the situation is not pleasant.[3]

Some representative values are shown in Table 3-1. Other factors can enter into a journey's comfort. These are often hard to quantify under the category of "amenities," using as a definition "the quality of being pleasing or agreeable." Pleasantness can include rest rooms, benches, scenery, and other distractions, and temperature control. Visual appeal may also be considered an amenity.[4]

Convenience

Convenience is a general term, but it has special meaning to a large and growing part of the traveling public, the handicapped passenger. This includes the infirm, the blind, the aged, and those with temporary handicaps due to accidents. Many transportation terminals apparently designed to serve all of the public have architectural barriers which limit or prevent their use by the handicapped. Sweden has legislation requiring that public facilities accommodate the handi-

Table 3-1
Passenger Comfort Criteria

	Noise	Warm	Cold
Physiological Boundary	120 db	110°	30°
Comfort	85 db	75°	65°

capped. The Stockholm subways provide a special funicular elevator for these persons. There is a series of required standards for federally funded housing projects in the United States, but the philosophy of designing for the handicapped has not 'been widely adopted in transportation facilities, with the exception of the BART system.[5]

Three subcategories discussed herein relate to this general term of "convenience"—escalators, better train service, and washrooms. In the first case, escalators are *not* necessarily the answer to the question of improving convenience in a rapid transit station, especially from the point of view of the handicapped or aged, as mentioned above. But they represent in this instance the attitude of the patron toward the *idea* of increased physical convenience. In this respect, the minimum criteria of the New York City Transit Authority for installation of an escalator are twenty-five feet of vertical rise, and four million passengers a year passing through the station.[6]

Better train service is introduced here for two reasons: from a broad point of view, a demand for better train service can be construed as a demand for greater convenience of travel, *assuming*, however, a *minimally acceptable level of service*; in other words, a consistently high ranking of that amenity factor would imply basically poor service. One-and-one-half-minute headways at peak hours are considered "acceptable"; twenty-minute headways at off-peak periods are considered "acceptable."

Washrooms and their adequacy or desirability are another "convenience" item considered here. In some systems, however, the question may be a moot one. Apparently the New York City Transit Authority has embarked upon a program of closing rest rooms. An extensive survey to determine the "least-used facilities" found that men used the facilities five to ten times more than women. In the borough of Queens the Transit Authority has permanently locked 50 rest rooms, of which 44 were for women. Currently in the same borough 116 are maintained: 77 for men and 39 for women. Some are open twenty-four hours a day, but most are open only from 7A.M. to 9 P.M.

An Authority official was quoted as saying, "They require extensive cleaning and maintenance and are frequently the scene of public nuisance." Some 20 percent of the city transit toilet facilities have thus been closed. In 1969 and 1970 some 702 crimes and 385 acts of vandalism were reported in the subway lavatories. Maintenance involves, normally, cleaning and disinfecting twice a day, and heavy cleaning once a week.[7] Since there is no statutory requirement for toilets at every station,[8] the Authority's actions are understandable.

Cleanliness

One source which defined certain variables for use in a "place benefit function" considers cleanliness as a "measure of the physical upkeep of the zone." The user gradually tends to look upon newly built, recently refurbished, or well-maintained environments as being desirable. Environments, in this case, mean physical appearance.

Cleanliness can also be considered as closely related to the ability of a transportation system to satisfy the status factor of modal choice. Most people relate cleanliness to efficiency, according to comments received.[9] The appeal of visual cleanliness seems to be more important than newness. National Analysis found that 69 percent of Washington, D.C. respondents emphasized cleanliness over "newness" for their proposed subway system. Aesthetics were found to be highly subjective, and deeply intertwined with environmental considerations.

As a measure of cleanliness, air pollution samples can be taken. One device measures only suspended particles, in terms of COH (coefficient of haze). The New York City Environmental Protection Administration's established scale of air quality in terms of COH is the following:

0 to 0.5	=	good
0.5 to 1.0	=	acceptable
1.0 to 1.6	=	unsatisfactory
1.6 to 8.3	=	unhealthy
greater than 8.3	=	dangerous

Table 3-2 gives tolerance levels in more specific terms. It may be assumed that gases are present in various degrees in a transportation system. Small concentrations of carbon disulfide (from 10 to 100 mg/m³), for instance, have been found to suppress the immunological responsiveness of an organism. The functions of the adrenal cortex have been suppressed in a study of such effects.[10]

However, the major problem in many transit systems is in the amount of particulates in the air. A recent report on the New York City subway system concluded that "particulate levels on station platforms . . . are greatly in excess of standards designed to protect public health." Another mentions "the possibility of a lead hazard."[11] But most of the "dirt" is ferretic material, and while the cleaning of tunnels is still a costly manual operation, the fact that steel dust is the major part of the problem leads to the need to develop a cleaning technique based on magnetic principles.[12]

Table 3-2
Respiration Safety Recommendations

MAXIMUM ALLOWABLE CONCENTRATION OF COMMON GASES, VAPORS, DUSTS,
AND FUMES IN THE BREATHING ATMOSPHERE

Dusts:[a]		Fluorine	0.1
Asbestos	5.0	Formaldehyde	20.0
Cement	15.0	Gasoline	500.0
Organic	50.0	Hydrochloric acid	10.0
Silica		Hydrogen chloride	5.0
above 50% free SiO_2	5.0	Hydrogen cyanide	20.0
5 to 50% free SiO_2	20.0	Hydrogen fluoride	3.0
below 5% free SiO_2	50.0	Hydrogen peroxide	1.0
Pottery	4.0	Hydrogen sulfide	20.0
Silicon carbide	50.0	Methyl alcohol (menthanol)	200.0
Mica		Methyl bromide	30.0
below 5% free SiO_2	20.0	Methyl chloride	500.0
Soapstone		Monochlorbenzine	75.0
below 5% free SiO_2	20.0	Naptha (coal tar)	200.0
Slate	15.0	Naptha (petroleum)	500.0
Portland cement	50.0	Nitric acid (fuming)	5.0
Talc	20.0	Nitrobenzene	5.0
Nuisance dust	50.0	Nitrogen dioxide	5.0
		Ozone	0.1
Gases and vapors:[b]		Phosgene	1.0
Acetone	1000.0	Phosphine	0.05
Ammonia, anhydrous	100.0	Phosphorus trichloride	1.0
Amyl acetate	200.0	Propyl alcohol (isopropyl alcohol)	400.0
Amyl alcohol	100.0	Sulfur dioxide	5.0
Analine	5.0	Tetrachlorethane	10.0
Arsine	1.0	Tetrachlorethylene	200.0
Bensene (benzol)	25.0	Tolual	200.0
Butenol	50.0	Trichlorethylene	200.0
Butyl acetate	20.0	Turpentine	100.0
Carbon disulfide	20.0	Xylol (coal-tar naptha)	100.0
Carbon dioxide	5000.0		
Carbon monoxide	100.0	Metallic dusts and fumes:[c]	
Carbon tetrachloride	25.0	Aluminum oxide	50.0
Chlorine	1.0	Cadmium	0.1
Chlorine trifluoride	0.1	Chromic acid	0.1
Chloroform	100.0	Lead (or lead compounds)	0.15
Dichlorobenzene	50.0	Manganese	6.0
Dichlorethyl ether	15.0	Mercury	0.1
Ether (ethyl)	400.0	Zinc Oxide	15.0

Table 3-2 (cont.)

Ethyl alcohol	1000.0	Chlorodiphenyl	1.0
Ethyl bromide	1700.0		
Ethyl chloride	70.0	Smoke:	
Ethylene dichloride	100.0	40% density (i.e., 60% light	
Ethylene oxide	50.0	visible through it)	

[a]Dusts: million parts per cubic foot. [b]Gases and vapors: parts per million. [c]Metallic dusts and fumes: milligrams per cubic meter.

Source: W.E. Woodson and D.W. Conover, *Human Engineering Guide for Equipment Designers* (2nd Ed.), originally published by the University of California Press, Berkeley, 1964; reprinted by permission of The Regents of the University of California.

Aesthetics

From the standpoint of terminals, "aesthetics" may be defined as "a high standard of architecture and graphics."[13] But this is perhaps too specific a definition for so subjective, vague, and general a subject. Another source uses the terminology "stimulus appeal," as "a measure of the existence of visual, auditory, olfactory, and tactile stimuli." This is an extremely relative measure, which will vary with each individual and the cultural background of the user.[14]

The aesthetic design of terminal interiors is the first thing that comes to mind when referring to visual design; but it is important to consider other visual impacts as well. Experienced terminal operators and designers are aware of certain human aspects of the traveling public, which psychologists might call the "travel anxiety syndrome." Passenger anxiety exists in varying degress, depending on the experience of the traveler. It is related to removal from the familiar surroundings and placement in a strange environment, where mistakes may cause delay and embarrassment. The terminal building space, its flow systems and directional signing, should be conceived to reduce this anxiety.

Color is one visual aspect of the terminal environment which has received little attention. Studies by color psychologists show that colors in the *red* end of the spectrum are "active" colors, exciting and disturbing the viewer and encouraging movement. The *blue* end of the spectrum is reportedly more relaxing, and conducive to concentration. There is a recorded case of an airline switching from a chartreuse aircraft interior after an unusual amount of air sickness was experienced with that color. The reported "relaxation and concentration" aspects of the blue end of the spectrum suggests that these colors may be more suited to the design of terminal interiors.[15]

Of course, colors can be pleasing or not, depending on combinations with other colors and with varying types of lighting. Tables 3-3 and 3-4 give "appearance ratings" and reflectance factors for different colors.

Table 3-3

Appearance Ratings of Colors Under Artificial Light Sources

Color	Daylight	Fluorescent Lamps				Incandescent Lamps
		Standard Cool White	Deluxe Cool White	Standard Warm White	Deluxe Warm White	
Maroon	Dull	Dull	Dull	Dull	Fair	Good
Red	Fair	Dull	Dull	Fair	Good	Good
Pink	Fair	Fair	Fair	Fair	Good	Good
Rust	Dull	Fair	Fair	Fair	Fair	Good
Orange	Dull	Dull	Fair	Fair	Fair	Good
Brown	Dull	Fair	Good	Good	Fair	Good
Tan	Dull	Fair	Good	Good	Fair	Good
Golden Yellow	Dull	Fair	Fair	Good	Fair	Good
Yellow	Dull	Fair	Good	Good	Dull	Fair
Olive	Good	Fair	Fair	Fair	Brown	Brown
Chartreuse	Good	Good	Good	Good	Yellowed	Yellowed
Dark Green	Good	Good	Good	Fair	Dull	Dull
Light Green	Good	Good	Good	Fair	Dull	Dull
Peacock Blue	Good	Good	Dull	Dull	Dull	Dull
Turquoise	Good	Fair	Dull	Dull	Dull	Dull
Royal Blue	Good	Fair	Dull	Dull	Dull	Dull
Light Blue	Good	Fair	Dull	Dull	Dull	Dull
Purple	Good	Fair	Dull	Dull	Good	Dull
Lavender	Good	Good	Dull	Dull	Good	Dull
Magenta	Good	Good	Fair	Dull	Good	Dull
Gray	Good	Good	Fair	Soft	Soft	Dull

Appearance Rating Key:

Good—Color appears most nearly as it would under an ideal white-light source, such as north skylight.

Fair—Color appears about as it would under an ideal white-light source, but is less vivid.

Dull—Color appears less vivid.

Brown—Color appears to be brown because of small amount of blue light emitted by lamp.

Yellowed—Color appears yellowed because of small amount of blue light emitted by lamp.

Soft—Surface takes on a pinkish cast because of red light emitted by lamp.

Source: W.E. Woodson and D.W. Conover, *Human Engineering Guide for Equipment Designers* (2nd Ed.), originally published by the University of California Press, Berkeley, 1964; reprinted by permission of The Regents of the University of California.

Table 3-4
Approximate Reflectance Factors for Various Surface Colors

Color	Amount of Reflected Light (%)	Color	Amount of Reflected Light (%)
White	85	Green	
		Light	65
Yellow		Medium	52
Light	75	Dark	7
Medium	65		
		Blue	
Buff		Light	55
Light	70	Medium	35
Medium	63	Dark	8
Gray		Red	
Light	75	Dark	13
Medium	55		
Dark	30	Brown	
		Dark	10

Source: W.E. Woodson and D.W. Conover, *Human Engineering Guide for Equipment Design* (2nd Ed.), originally published by the University of California Press, Berkeley, 1964; reprinted by permission of The Regents of the University of California.

A trend toward more attractive subways may have begun with the design of the Toronto subway, opened in 1954. The first completed system to strongly emphasize aesthetics, the Montreal Metro, which opened in 1967, has earned such praise as the following, from *The Architectural Forum:*

Montreal farmed out the design of different stations to different architects, with the result that some stations are breathtakingly beautiful. . . . The most breathtaking of all is Place Bonaventure, located under the vast merchandise mart of the same name . . . great vaults reminiscent of Piranesi, washes of light largely from concealed sources, handsome finished and smooth details . . . it's the best subway in North America, and the one to which all others will, henceforth, have to measure up.[16]

The problems of refurbishing existing, older subways are much greater. Little has been done in this regard because of limited funds. For instance, current practice of the New York City Transit Authority is to paint on a ten-year cycle.[17] While initial construction may not be any more costly for good design, cosmetic alterations of existing structures are expensive and meet a good deal of resistance among transit operators. Aided by a HUD grant, the Massachusetts Bay Transportation Authority began a station modernization program "to provide modern facilities which will be consistent with a rising standard of urban living, make transit riding more convenient and pleasant for existing customers and [for new riders]." The MBTA planners indicate that on the facilities which "the customers see continually, attention is being paid . . . to improving functional efficiency and visual impact through good design."[18]

There is simply very little literature which discussed public transit facility design.

Temperature

Human comfort requires the maintenance of proper temperature and humidity. Other aspects of comfort may include such factors as acoustical shielding from noise, special ventilation where passengers are exposed to vehicular fumes, and weather protection.[19]

"Weather control" has been defined as the "ability of a person to have control over weather environmental variables to some degree," using artificial devices, but it can include the provision of some direct or indirect protection from active weather elements (wind, rain, snow). It does not necessarily mean total personal control over weather elements, but it does mean some influence over protection from the elements.[20]

While the effects of good temperature on human performance are not completely understood, certain generalizations have been made. "Ideal work conditions" for most Americans have been set between 63 and 70 degrees Fahrenheit, with humidity between 30 and 70 percent, for "light work."[21] A more extensive breakdown of levels is given in Table 3-5.

In addition, the extremities are considered in Table 3-6, in which the temperature of the body parts, not the contacting air, are related to comfort levels.

Figures 3-1, 3-2, and 3-3 give the comfort levels of temperature as related to relative humidity, and tolerance of heat as related to time exposure. It is desirable to stay within these ranges, but it is not always possible or practical. Acclimatization over a period of time can help overcome some of the discom-

Table 3-5
Significant Temperature Levels

120° F	Tolerable for about 1 hour, but is far above physical or mental activity range (160° F for 1/2 hour)
85° F	Mental activities slow down, slow response, errors begin
75° F	Physical fatigue begins
65° F	Optimum condition
50° F	Physical stiffness of extremities begins
65° to 75° F	Summer comfort zone
63° to 71° F	Winter comfort zone

Source: W.E. Woodson and D.W. Conover, *Human Engineering Guide for Equipment Design* (2nd Ed.), originally published by The University of California Press, Berkeley, 1964, p. 2-226; reprinted by permission of The Regents of The University of California.

34

Table 3-6
Relation Between Comfort and Temperature of the Extremities

	(Degrees F)	
	Hands	Feet
Minimum	68	73
Tolerable	68-59	73-64
Intolerable pain	59-50	64-55
Numbness	50-	55-

Source: W.E. Woodson and D.W. Conover, *Human Engineering Guide for Equipment Design* (2nd Ed.), originally published by the University of California Press, Berkeley, 1964, p. 2-227; reprinted by permission of The Regents of the University of California.

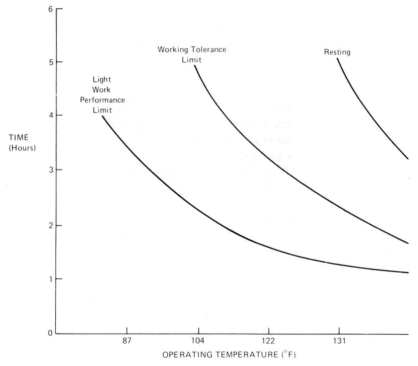

Figure 3-1. Tolerance to Heat. Source: W.E. Woodson and D.W. Conover, *Human Engineering Guide for Equipment Designers*, (2nd Ed.), originally published by the University of California Press, Berkeley, 1964, p. 2-227; reprinted by permission of The Regents of the University of California.

Figure 3-2. Temperature-Humidity Comfort Zone. Source: W.E. Woodson and D.W. Conover, *Human Engineering Guide for Equipment Designers*, (2nd Ed.), originally published by the University of California Press, Berkeley, 1964, p. 2-227; reprinted by permission of The Regents of the University of California.

fort, particularly for heat, but time spent in subway stations or trains may not be long enough for this acclimatization. In general, radiant heating is better than hot air heating, which causes a feeling of staleness. *Ventilation* is extremely important in trains and stations, to help maintain proper temperature and humidity, and to keep CO_2 levels below a certain level (see Tables 3-7 and 3-8). *Heat* can have appreciable deleterious effects on humans. One study found a reduction in task capabilities as heat went from 63 to 99 degrees F.[22] Another found the prolonged exposure to temperature fluctuations resulted in a reduction in the concentration of proteins in the blood, a reduction in amino acid nitrogen in the serum; a general denaturation process in the body.[23]

Other studies have confirmed these phenomena. In one, oxygen consumption rose, heart rate rose, and there were increases in volumes of plasma, extracellular space, and total body water.[24] In another, mental performance was impaired.[25] There are even different effects on the sexes; studies show that women have a higher sweat onset threshold, lower sweating capacity, and a lower level of acclimatization (lower endurance) in very hot conditions.[26]

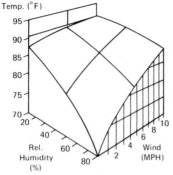

The curved surface on the chart at the left represents the "comfort" line. It illustrates how changes in any one of the parameters can maintain a comfort level. For example, with no air movement, comfort exists with temperature at 72° and humidity at 90 per cent. Temperature can rise to 75°, with humidity still at 90 per cent, if the air is caused to move at 2 mph, because the subject still "feels comfortable."

Figure 3-3. Temperature-Humidity and Air Flow. Source: W.E. Woodson and D.W. Conover, *Human Engineering Guide for Equipment Designers,* (2nd Ed.), originally published by the University of California Press, Berkeley, 1964, p. 2-228; reprinted by permission of The Regents of the University of California.

Table 3-7
Typical Commercial Ventilation Rate Recommendations

A   1 cu. ft. fresh air per minute per square foot of floor space (average workroom)

B   1½ cu. ft. fresh air per minute for heavy work (except when net free space per worker = cu. ft., reduce this amount by 50 per cent)

C   ½ cu. ft. fresh air per minute per square foot of floor space (average office)

Other typical areas:

Department stores, auditoriums, libraries, schoolrooms, churches, courtrooms, gymnasiums _____ use B

Museums, railroad station _____ use C

Hospitals _____ use A

Operating rooms, lavatories, laboratories _____ use 2 cubic feet

Kitchens _____ use 4 cubic feet

Source: W.E. Woodson and D.W. Conover, *Human Engineering Guide for Equipment Designers* (2nd Ed.) originally published by the University of California Press, Berkeley 1964, p. 2-228; reprinted by permission of The Regents of the University of California.

Of course, the widespread and increasing use of air conditioning in homes, offices, and commercial establishments, as well as in other modes of transportation, has made the public even less tolerant, psychologically, of the level of discomfort common to many transit systems in the summertime. It is not uncommon for temperatures on a subway station platform to be at least 20

Table 3-8
Necessary Ventilation Rate

	Oxygen Consumption Per Person at Sea Level (cu. ft. per min.)	Ventilation Rate for Person to Maintain Concentration of CO_2 Below 0.5 Percent (cu. ft. per min.)			
		Sea Level	5000 Ft.	10,000 Ft.	15,000 Ft.
At rest	0.008	1.2	1.4	1.7	2.1
Moderate activity	0.028	3.9	4.7	6.7	6.9
Vigorous activity	0.056	8.7	9.7	11.7	14.5

Source: W.E. Woodson and D.W. Conover, *Human Engineering Guide for Equipment Designers* (2nd Ed.), originally published by the University of California Press, Berkeley, 1964, p. 2-229; reprinted by permission of The Regents of the University of California.

degrees warmer than the outdoor temperature. Figure 3-4 shows the extent of typical variations which have occurred during a twelve-month period in New York City.

A gradual increase in temperature of subway tunnels and stations has occurred during the past few years in several subway systems throughout the world. This has led to considerable passenger discomfort, especially during summer and fall months. In early subway systems, an increase in underground temperature was usually traced to inadequate ventilation. However, the more recent temperature increases have been generally attributed to more frequent service, with heavier and faster cars. The electrical energy supplied for car propulsion, heating, air conditioning, and lighting eventually ends up as heat in the subway and the surrounding substructure and the nearby soil. This heat, in addition to that resulting from the passengers, must be removed by circulation of outdoor air. The surrounding earth does not serve as a strong heat sink, but acts mainly to minimize air temperature variations.

The greatest source of heat in the subway is the electrical energy required for the propulsion and braking of the train. Other heat sources from electrical energy include car and station auxiliary equipment, fans, and lighting. All electrical energy supplied to the system is ultimately dissipated in the form of heat. Passengers also contribute metabolic energy to the system. Each passenger contributes about 600 Btu/hr of heat.

Ventilation removes a good part of this heat, although some is temporarily stored in the tunnel structure and surrounding environment, and is generally returned to the subway air when the weather becomes cooler.

Subway conditions are therefore dependent on past history because of this thermal storage capacity of the subway structures and surrounding earth. Conditions are also affected by train traffic, passenger traffic, external temperatures, and humidity. Humidity has a substantial effect on passenger comfort. Its

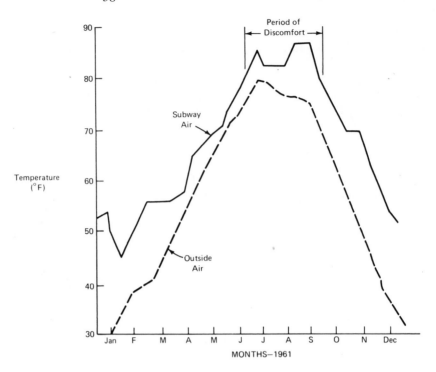

Figure 3-4. Comparison of Station and Outdoor Air Temperatures. Source: W. Lassow, E.L. Lustenader, and K. Schoch, *A Thermal Model for the Evaluation of Subway Ventilation and Air Conditioning*, ASCE-ASME National Transportation Engineering Meeting, Seattle, Washington, July 26-30, 1971.

principal sources include external air, metabolic energy, seepage of moisture through the walls, and drainage of rainfall from the street. Its primary method of removal is ventilation.

The characteristics of the subway which make it different from the majority of air-conditioning applications are short-term occupancy and high-density passenger loading. The subway application appears to be unique, particularly with regard to the second factor. Unfortunately, comfort criteria data directly applicable to the subway situation seem to be nonexistent. Data developed by the American Society of Heating, Refrigeration and Air-conditioning Engineers (ASHRAE) could be said to apply more to long-term occupancy, and low occupant density.

The average time a passenger rides in the subway is 20 to 30 minutes, and the average time spent waiting on the platform is much shorter. This period of occupancy is within the normal definition of short-term occupancy, or 15 to 40 minutes. Of course, this is an *average* time and does not greatly reflect actual individual experience.

The relationship between dry bulb temperature, relative humidity, and effective temperature for "still" air (velocity less than 20 feet per minute) is shown in Figure 3-5. At 100 percent relative humidity, the effective temperature is the same as the dry bulb temperature. At moderate temperature (70 to 80 degrees F.) and relative humidities (near 50 percent), the effect of increasing air velocities is about a one-point decrease in effective temperature for each 100-foot-per-minute increase in air velocity, up to 400 feet per minute.

Summer comfort data developed by ASHRAE for long-term occupancy in "still" air are presented in Figure 3-6. These data are applicable to United States residents at about the latitude of New York City. This figure shows the percent of the population that would be comfortable at various effective temperatures. About 97 percent of the people are comfortable at an effective temperature of

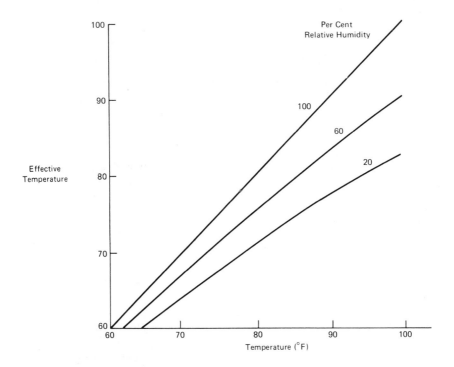

Figure 3-5. Effective Temperatures. Source: W. Lassow, E.L. Lustenader, and K. Schoch, *A Thermal Model for the Evaluation of Subway Ventilation and Air Conditioning*, ASCE-ASME National Transportation Engineering Meeting, Seattle, Washington, July 26-30, 1971.

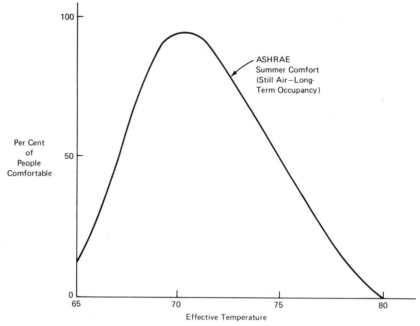

Figure 3-6. Summer Comfort vs. Effective Temperature. Source: W. Lassow, E.L. Lustenader, and K. Schoch, *A Thermal Model for the Evaluation of Subway Ventilation and Air Conditioning*, ASCE-ASME National Transportation Engineering Meeting, Seattle, Washington, July 26-30, 1971.

70 to 71 degrees. This is the optimum condition in normal operation. Only 50 percent are comfortable at 75 degrees. It is suggested that this temperature should not be exceeded except under unusual circumstances and then only for a few hours per year.

Noise

Noise is another major problem in transportation systems, and one which of course will cost money to correct. In the purely economic sense, a balance is reached when the equivalent yearly cost of an increase in noise control devices and procedures becomes greater than the increased net annual income that would result from increased patronage and reduced community complaints.[27]

When complaints are such that lost revenue and lawsuits cost more than added noise control, noise reduction becomes worthwhile on a purely economic cost-effectiveness basis (Figure 3-7). However, from a logical, human, responsible point of view, the purely economic considerations must give way to the concept of "community values."

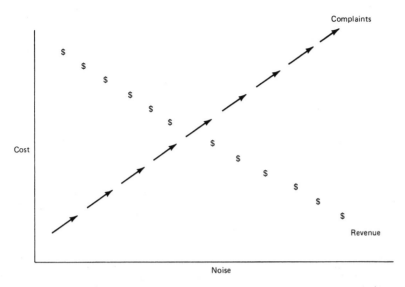

Figure 3-7. Noise/Cost Ratio. Source: V. Salmon, "Noise in Mass-Transit Systems," in *Stanford Research Institute Journal*, No. 16, Sept. 1967.

Noise has been defined as a "true operating characteristic of an engineered device," as real as power, strength, or speed. It can be defined, measured, contained, prevented, and even legislated against. What is certainly important is that acoustics experts have a good idea of how much noise can be tolerated from an annoyance standpoint, or from a legal liability standpoint.[28]

Noise is "the tribute we pay for progress."[29] Customers react against excessive noise, when it is within their power, by using other modes of transportation. It is a major problem on subway systems around the world (Table 3-9). For the complex sounds of a rapid transit system, ORI performed a frequency analysis by taking sound pressure readings in discrete frequency bands.[30] From these readings, the "loudness level" was computed. One common unit of measure of the loudness of a sound is the *phon*, a measure of the loudness of a sound as judged by the human ear.

Twelve field tests were conducted *inside rail vehicles* in Berlin, Hamburg, Lisbon, London, Paris, Paris (rubber-tired), Stockholm, Toronto, Boston, Chicago, New York, and Philadelphia. Also, tests were made inside a city bus in Washington, a low-center-of-gravity intercity Talgo train in Madrid, and a rubber-tired experimental guided vehicle in Milan.

Quantification of the social value of decreased noise is a factor in the

Table 3-9
Noise Measurement Data in Subway Stations

System	Avg. Sound Pressure Level (db)			Avg. Loudness Level (phons)		
	Arrival	Stop	Departure	Arrival	Stop	Departure
Chicago	100	78	92	106	82	99
New York	100	75	98	108	78	103
Toronto	87	81	87	96	84	93
Berlin	94	73	88	98	82	92
Hamburg	97	78	88	105	81	95
Lisbon	105	88	104	110	94	109
Paris (rubber)	88	65	96	101	68	93
Paris (steel wheel)	99	77	96	108	81	106
Stockholm	96	82	93	103	89	100

Source: E.W. Davis. *Comparison of Noise and Vibration Levels in Rapid Transit Vehicle Systems*, Operations Research, Inc., April 1964.

cost-effectiveness evaluation procedure. But it is difficult to estimate the reactions of people to noise, and the weighting of such a factor in a problem. The word "noise" refers to both the *sensation* and the *physical stimulus* associated with it. The most common measure used is *perceived noise decibels*. The decibel (db) is a physical measure of the intensity of a noise; *perceived noise decibels* (PNdb) describe the "annoyance" of the noise. There is a doubling of "loudness" every 10 db. Common noise levels can be listed as shown in Table 3-10.

For most people, a change of two or three PNdb is a *just noticeable* change in annoyance.[31]

Annoyance increases with loudness and the amount of high-pitched sound in the noise. This is why a squeal is more annoying than a roar. Therefore, the

Table 3-10
Common Noise Levels

Source	Loudness Level db (A)
Soft whisper at 5 feet	34
Inside small car at 30 mph	70
Oxford St. London (busy thoroughfare)	76
Edge of limited-access freeway	90

Source: K.M. Solomon, R.J. Solomon and J.S. Silien, *Passenger Psychological Dynamics*, Journal of Urban Transportation Corp. and ASCE, New York, 1968. Table 3.2.0-1.

higher-pitched (high-frequency) components should be weighted more heavily than the lower-pitched ones.

The PNdb should be weighted by amounts corresponding to various psychological factors. Pure tones (such as wheel squeal on curves) are more annoying than "smooth" noise. Sound that is sudden, repeated noise, and nighttime noise are also more annoying. When the person annoyed can *see* the noise source or feel its vibrations, the sense of intrusion is reinforced, and increased annoyance is reported.[32]

With mass transportation passengers, the complaint of excessive noise will often be based on "speech interference." From standard noise rating (NR) curves, a number is obtained that characterizes the speech interference expected. At NR 60 speech is intelligible at two feet. For underground station-platform noise, the limit should probably be set at NR 70.[33]

If wheels and rails are of steel, and rolling stock is poorly maintained, the noise level can increase as much as 15 PNdb from this cause alone. A common support noise is wheel squeal on curves. This remains a largely unsolved problem. In a railed vehicle it is possible to reduce support noise by special wheels.

The passenger is closest to the noise source, and receives a concentrated and almost continuous exposure during his trip. For the passenger on the platform of an underground station, an effective means of noise control is to wall off the platform from the tracks. Because the required attenuation of the wall is only 25 to 30 db, its construction need not be expensive.

This useful noise-control device is called an "acoustic parapet," an absorbent-lined wall on both sides of each vehicle path (Figure 3-8). The higher the wall and the smaller the clearance to the vehicle, the greater the noise reduction. For closely fitting parapets extending up to just below window height, the radiated noise can be reduced as much as 15 db. On curves the value of the parapets is reduced, because their clearance must be much larger than on the straightaway.[34]

It has been suggested that large amounts of absorption be used near the tunnel opening. This would be graded to zero in a few hundred feet.

As to noise levels, continued exposure, for instance, to 80 db can bring loss of hearing.[35] Noise, in fact, can "drive you crazy," or "kill," according to one source.[36] But there is little known about the level of background noise that people can tolerate.[37] In the United States, 11 million adults and 3 million children suffer from some hearing loss. A certain proportion of these can be attributed to excessive noise.[38] The major sources of noise pollution in cities are: transportation, building construction, and street repair.[39]

Short-duration noise of low frequency, up to 150 db, is within human tolerance.[40] But the higher the noise level (intensity), the greater the decrement in degree of performance. Sudden increases in stimulation may produce behavioral aberrations.[41] Man can adapt within from several minutes to 1 1/2 to 2 hours, depending on the intensity of the noise. There is apparently no damage

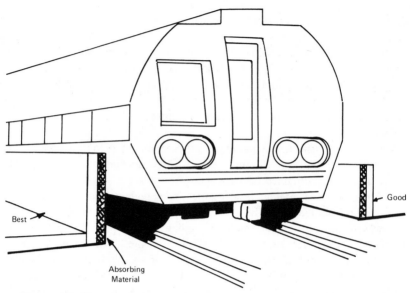

Figure 3-8. Use of the "Acoustic Parapet". Source: V. Salmon, "Noise in Mass-Transit Systems," in *Stanford Research Institute Journal*, No. 16, Sept. 1967.

to the ear with constant levels of noise up to 10 db at any frequency. The maximum levels of sonic pressures at frequencies of 200, 600, 1250, and 4000 Hertz (cycles per second) correspond to db levels of 100 and 90, 90 and 85, 85 and 75, 75 and 65, respectively. These are levels characteristic of many industries. But tests show a lowering of hearing sensitivity after noise of intensities corresponding to 100, 90, 85, and 75 db.[42]

The boundary between harmful and neutral effects depends on the phenomenon of sensitivity after noise of intensities of 90, 85, 75, and 65 db, with maximum levels of sonic energy corresponding to 200, 600, 1250, and 4000 Hertz.

The average shift of thresholds of audibility is 5 db, with sensitivity restored in less than three minutes.

The fatiguing effects with shifts to 100, 90, 85, and 75 db and the same cps indicate a shift of audibility thresholds of 15 db. Sensitivity is restored in more than 10 minutes.

Effects on the heart are shown in Table 3-11. Noise combinations of 100, 90, 85, and 75 db at 200, 600, 1250, and 4000 Hertz are described as *unpleasant, confusing, irritating*, and *hardly bearable*. There is a blocking, and ringing of ears, headache, and exhaustion. But the effects are not the same for each individual. There are also disturbances of hemodynamics.

Table 3-11
Effects of Noise on the Heart

Spectrum of Noise	Maximum Level of Sonic Energy cps	Intensity db	Difference Relative to Initial Magnitudes	
			Diastole (sec)	Pulse Rate (1 min.)
Low Frequency	200	100	+0.20	−14
		90	+ .12	− 7
Average	600	90	+ .17	−11
		85	+ .06	− 4
High	1250	85	+ .18	−15
		75	+ .10	−10
High	400	75	+ .17	−12
		65	+ .04	− 3

Standards should be set at between 62.5 and 4000 Hertz, so as to have no bad effects. This is established at 95 db at 62.5 cps, and 65 db at 4000 Hertz, as shown in Figure 3-9.

There are of course people with greater sensitivity to noise than others. But noise is harmless to the human organism as far as permanent damage is

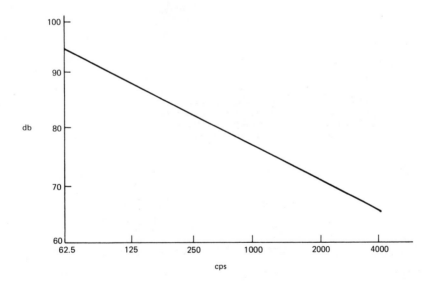

Figure 3-9. Acceptable Combinations of db and cps. Source: A.A. Arkad' Yevshiy, "Hygienic Standards for Constant Noise in Industry," in *Gigiyena: Sanitorya* No. 7, Moscow, July 1964.

concerned at 90, 85, 75, 65 db with 200, 600, 1250, 4000 Hertz, while intensities of 100, 90, 85, 75 db have a fatiguing effect on the organism.[43]

Tables 3-12 and 3-13 give maximum allowable sound levels, by octave bands, and length of exposure, to avoid hearing loss. Temporary hearing losses resulting from noise exposures are greater the higher the noise level, the longer the duration of exposure, and, within limits, the shorter the bandwidth within which the energy is concentrated. The effect is seen as a loss in auditory acuity, especially between 1000 and 6000 Hertz, and as a reduction in the loudness of sound. For example, a 15-db loss in sensitivity to octave-bandwidth sounds can

Table 3-12
Limits for Deafness—Avoidance and Comfort

| | Maximum Permissible Sound Pressure Level (db above 0.0002 microbar) | | | |
| | Deafness-Avoidance Criterion | | Comfort Criterion | |
Octave Band	Occasional Exposure (1 hour or less)	Repeated Exposure (period of months)	Noisy (people expect noise)	Quiet (people expect quiet)
38-75	125	115	100	80
75-150	120	110	95	70
150-300	120	110	90	60
300-600	120	105	85	55
600-1200	115	100	75	50
1200-2400	110	95	65	50
2400-4800	105	90	60	50
4800-9600	110	95	55	45

Source: W.E. Woodson and D.W. Conover, *Human Engineering Guide for Equipment Designers* (2nd Ed.), originally published by the University of California Press, Berkeley, 1964, p. 2-224; reprinted by permission of The Regents of the University of California.

Table 3-13
Noise Limits for Avoiding Hearing Damage—db

Time	Ears Unprotected	With Ear Plugs	Ear Plugs and Muffs
8 hrs.	100	112	120
1 hr.	108	120	128
5 min.	120	132	140
30 sec.	130	142	150

Source: W.E. Woodson and D.W. Conover, *Human Engineering Guide for Equipment Designers* (2nd Ed.), originally published by the University of California Press, Berkeley, 1964, p. 2-225; reprinted by permission of The Regents of the University of California.

follow exposure to steady-state octave-band pressure levels of 100 db. The loss in sensitivity to pure tones at and above 1000 Hertz following the same conditions might be of the order of 35 db. The loss is greatest for people with normal hearing.

Temporary hearing losses are produced rapidly, and are maximum within about seven minutes for exposure to pure tones. Maximum loss from wide-band noise is longer, and depends on whether or not it is steady-state noise. For steady-state noise in an industrial setting containing octave-band pressure levels of 90-100 db, an average loss in auditory acuity of 15 db for tones above 1000 Hertz can be expected following a four-hour exposure. Exposure to nonsteady and intermittent noise of the same level has a lesser effect; a full working day of exposure to this kind of environment is required to produce an average temporary hearing loss of 5 db at frequencies above 1000 Hertz.

Recovery from temporary hearing loss depends on the duration of exposure, the nature of the sound, and the age of the person affected. Recovery of nonimpulsive sounds might require two to five times the duration of the exposure, depending on the nature of the sound. For example, normal workday exposure to octave-band levels of 95 db might require two to five days for complete recovery of normal auditory acuity, particularly in the 1000-6000 Hertz region, and a thirty-minute exposure to a pure tone of 105 db might require two to three hours for complete recovery. The fact that the major losses are primarily within the region of speech sounds has serious implications for speech-communication systems.[44]

Legislation against excessive noise levels is of course needed. Congress, in 1971, was wrestling with the need for control. William D. Ruckelshaus, head of the Environmental Protection Agency, estimated the time required estimated the time required to set national standards in three primary sources—transportation vehicles, construction equipment, and other internal-combustion-engine vehicles—as 15 to 18 months. He stated that there was "no doubt" that noise affects the public health and impairs the quality of modern life. He indicated that some "20 percent of the population, in addition to those exposed to occupational noises, have significant hearing impairment by age 50 to 59."[45]

The State of New Jersey has "upgraded" harmful noise from a misdemeanor to a state offense punishable by a fine up to $3000,[46] and, at this writing, the New York City Council is considering a similar measure fixing decibel limits.

This recognition of the need for noise control is international. It was most recently expressed in Moscow, for instance, as a clamor on the part of the public for greater production of ear plugs.[47]

The New York City Transit Authority recognized the following sources of noise in the subway system:

wheel on rail
wheels on curves

rail irregularities
structure and equipment
construction

Methods of control include:

lubricating rail on curves
resilient track fasteners
maintenance and grinding of rail
track on "floating slab"
acoustic material on tunnel walls
acoustic material in fan and vent ducts[48]

Noise limits set by the federal government's Occupational Safety and Health Act of 1970 specify 80 db as an occupational noise limit (see Table 3-14).[49]

Another source sets forth "ideal interior noise levels" as shown in Table 3-15.[50]

Table 3-14
Permissible Noise Exposure

Duration/Day, Hrs.	Sound Level, dbA
8	90
6	92
4	95
3	97
2	100
1½	102
1	105
½	110
¼ or less	115

Table 3-15
Ideal Interior Noise Levels

Nature of Premises	Noise Levels in db	
	Day	Night
Quiet offices	55	—
Busy offices	68	—
Dwellings in a busy urban area	50	35

Source: K.M. Solomon, R.J. Solomon and J.S. Silien, *Passenger Psychological Dynamics*, Journal of Urban Transportation Corp. and ASCE, New York, 1968, Table 3.2.2-1.

Vibration is another problem which can have deleterious effects on man. Solid-borne vibration can have strong effects.[51] Low-frequency vibration, the limit for easy perception, is at one inch/sec/sec, or about 1/400 the acceleration due to gravity. There are no established limits for vibration tolerance. But amplitudes smaller than 1/1000 of an inch, at frequencies over 10 Hertz, are a genuine source of annoyance. An acceleration of vibration of 0.01g is noticeable. If it is equal to .04 to .05g it is distinctly unpleasant.[52]

The human body reacts to vibration and resonating stimuli much the same as does a mechanical system of masses and springs. When the resonant stimulus approximates the natural human-body resonance of about 5 Hertz, the person concerned finds this quite disagreeable.

Resonant frequency of the human body should be considered in the design of vehicles and vehicle seating; i.e., avoid amplifying the effect on the body, by damping. Limits suggested are:

> pelvic region, 4-6 Hertz
> abdominal mass, 4-8 Hertz
> head (relative to shoulders), 30 Hertz

(see Figure 3-10 and Table 3-16).[53]

Acceleration and deceleration rates are another area of passenger comfort which should enter into consideration in further studies. Recognized boundaries of "comfort" and "discomfort" are 0.1g and 1.0g, respectively.[54]

Illumination

Items to consider in illumination are:

> the distribution of light in the area
> the brightness contrasts of viewed objects and details
> the quality and color of the illuminants and work-place surface
> the intensity of illumination.[55]

Tables 3-17 and 3-18 summarize information on this subject.

The New York City Transit Authority considers 10 foot-candles "adequate."[56] A more acceptable standard would be 15.

Safety and Security

Safety can be considered "related to vitality yet basic in itself." The desire for safety and survival is so basic that it is beyond debate. Yet many aspects of

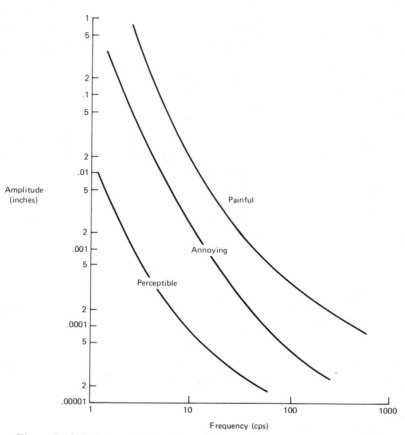

Figure 3-10. Levels of Vibration. Source: W.E. Woodson and D.W. Conover, *Human Engineering Guide for Equipment Designers* (2nd Ed.), originally published by the University of California Press, Berkeley, 1964, p. 2-234; reprinted by permission of The Regents of the University of California.

public transportation in urban areas work against safety as a primary goal. Most stations "contain features which contribute to the lack of safety."[57] Specific design characteristics underscore this negative environment: blind corners, minimal lighting, confining waiting rooms, and dark pedestrian ways.

Security can certainly be increased through the obvious availability of police officers, and the use of currently available surveillance and communications technology. The New York City Transit Authority's two-way radio system is, in concept at least, the kind of thing necessary to restore confidence in personal safety for rapid transit riders and drivers.[58]

Security is very important to mental ease or comfort. *Actual* security of a

Table 3-16
Typical Effects of Vibration on Human Beings

Response	Effect[a]	Frequency (cps)	Displacement (inches)
Respiration control	−	3.5–6.0	.75
	−	4.0–8.0	.14–.61
Body tremor	+	40.0	.065
	+	70.0	.03
Hand tremor	+	20.0	.015–.035
	+	25.0	.035–.055
	+	30–300	.02–.20
	+	1000	.008
Aiming	−	15.0	.07–.12
	−	25.0	.035–.055
	−	35.0	.03–.05
Hand coordination	−	2.5–3.5	.50
Foot pressure constancy	−	2.5–3.5	.50
Hand reaction time	+	2.5–3.5	.50
Visual acuity	−	1.0–24	.024–.588
	−	35.0	.03–.05
	−	40.0	.065
	−	70.0	.03
	−	2.5–3.5	.5
Tracking	−	1.0–50	.05–.18
	−	2.5–3.5	.5
Attention	−	2.5–3.5	.5
	−	30–300	.02–.20

[a]+ = increase, − = degrades
Source: W.E. Woodson and D.W. Conover, *Human Engineering Guide for Equipment Designers* (2nd Ed.), originally published by the University of California Press, Berkeley, 1964, p. 2-234; reprinted by permission of The Regents of the University of California.

transportation system or place is not easily recognized by users. However, *perceived* security is usually recognizable, such as providing good lighting, well-marked pedestrian pathways, etc. Therefore, security should be measured in terms of *the way users see security; perceptually.*[59] Since the policeman is part of the *perception* of security, this is the measure which can be used in evaluating patron opinion.

Safety in public transportation was once taken for granted because mass transit's accident record had always been better than the private automobile's. But consideration of safety today includes exposures to assaults and robberies either on transit vehicles or in stations. This factor is quite significant, because it inhibits off-peak patronage.[60]

Table 3-17
General Illumination Levels

Task Condition	Level (foot-candles)	Type of Illumination
Small detail, low contrast, prolonged periods, high speed, extreme accuracy	100	Supplementary type of lighting. Special fixture such as desk lamp.
Small detail, fair contrast, close work, speed not essential	50-100	Supplementary type of lighting.
Normal desk and office-type work	20-50	Local, lighting. Ceiling fixture directly overhead.
Recreational tasks that are not prolonged	10-20	General lighting. Random room light, either natural or artificial
Seeing not confined, contrast good, object fairly large	5-10	General lighting.
Visibility for moving about, handling large objects	2-5	General or supplementary

Source: W.E. Woodson and D.W. Conover, *Human Engineering Guide for Equipment Designers* (2nd Ed.) originally published by the University of California Press, Berkeley 1964, p. 2-228; reprinted by permission of The Regents of the University of California.

Of course, "safety" is a relative measure of perceived physical safety in an area that protects the user from possible detrimental effects from encounters with his environment: moving vehicles, stationary objects, or population types perceived to be physically hostile. In most instances, perceived safety is directly related to the time of day (e.g., lack of light decreases perceived security).[61] For this reason, opinion surveys would have to be made at both peak and off-peak hours, to gain insight into changes in perception of the importance of the various amenities.

Synergistic Effects

Human beings are rarely exposed to a single environmental stress. More typically, they are exposed to some combination of stresses, such as temperature and humidity, temperature and noise, vibration and noise, or vibration, noise, and acceleration.

It has been demonstrated that synergism may occur when environmental stresses are combined. Megel found that combinations of heat and vibration can become lethal to rats, although neither stress is lethal by itself.[62]

Synergism does not necessarily occur when environmental stresses are combined. This is particularly true for human performance.

Noise and heat are one combination of environmental stresses encountered in many situations in which synergism might be expected to occur. There has been

Table 3-18
Specific Recommendations, Illumination Levels

Location	Level (foot-candles)	Location	Level (foot-candles)
Home:		School:	
Reading	40	On Chalkboards	50
Writing	40	Desks	30
Sewing	75-100	Drawing (art)	50
Kitchen	50	Gyms	20
Mirror (shaving)	50	Auditorium	10
Laundry	40	Theater:	
Games	40	Lobby	20
Workbench	50	During intermission	5
General	10 or more	During movie	0.1
Office:		Passenger train:	
Bookkeeping	50	Reading, writing	20-40
Typing	50	Dining	15
Transcribing	40	Steps, vestibules	10
General correspondence	30	Doctor's office:	
Filing	30	Examination room	100
Reception	20	Dental-surgical	200
		Operating table	1800

Source: W.E. Woodson and D.W. Conover, *Human Engineering Guide for Equipment Designers* (2nd Ed.) originally published by the University of California Press, Berkeley 1964, p. 2-228; reprinted by permission of The Regents of the University of California.

some discussion in the literature of the suppression of pain associated with high-intensity noise.[63]

One of the leading theories of thermal sensation is that warmth is sensed from the dilation of the peripheral blood vessels, and cooling from the constriction of the same blood vessels.[64] It has been postulated, therefore, that any agent producing constriction of the peripheral blood vessels should also produce a cooling sensation. High-intensity noise could be considered such an agent, since noise produces an overall arousal of the sympathetic nervous system. One part of this arousal is constriction of the peripheral blood vessels.

Since noise constricts the peripheral blood vessels, it should also produce a cooling sensation.[65] It was believed that noise might alleviate the discomfort of heat by producing a sensation of cooling, but at the cost of interfering with thermal equilibrium; but no evidence was found that noise alleviates the discomfort of heat. On the contrary, noise was found to increase the heart and respiratory rates.[66]

Another combination is *vibration and noise*. The influence of total *vertical vibrations* at a frequency of 70 cps, and an amplitude of 0.4 mm, reduces by an average of one-third to one-half the qualitative accomplishment of an experimental task. *Noise* at 90 db cuts qualitative accomplishment an average of one-half. But the deepest and most persistent reduction of mental efficiency is caused by the combination of *vibration and noise*. The longer the exposure, the greater the reduction of mental efficiency. *Vibration* is the stronger component.[67]

An exhaustive review of the literature suggests that there are no recommended standards of prevalent combinations of factors.

**Part II
Developing an Allocation
Technique and Real-life
Test Values**

4

An Allocation Technique

Development of the Technique

An ideal allocation index, or model, developed from the preferences of the riding public, must rate the importance of improving amenities; modify this by considerations of environmental and human factors comfort levels (and the proximity of existing conditions to those levels); and further modify it by economic factors (incremental cost of improvement to reach comfort levels). An "exposure" weighting, based on numbers of patrons using a specific facility, can also be introduced. Minimum requirements include, therefore:

1. *Public opinion preference ranking* (and rating) of a given set of improvements, or amenities.
2. Knowledge of *a set of average comfort or acceptance levels* of those amenities, including meaningful incremental units for each.
3. *Unit cost of improvement* for each variable, or amenity factor, again on the basis of meaningful incremental units.

The *exposure* weighting, for choices among facilities, would comprise the number of patrons per day for a particular station.

Method of Analysis

A priority ranking, from a patron opinion survey, is developed for each of n *amenity factors*. After normalizing these to percentage values, they may be represented as R_i, where $i = 1, 2, \ldots, n$.

R_i is thus the original patron ranking, i.e., an index number, in its own right, of need for amenity improvement, by *need*, and by *cost*.

A series of meaningful increments is then developed for each factor, and tabulated. Each increment represents a clearly distinguishable unit of public recognition, with the lowest level corresponding to a patently undesirable state, and the highest level equal to "comfort," or acceptability. The jth increment (*level*) of the ith factor will be represented by f_{ij} ($i = 1, 2, \ldots, n$ and $j = 1, 2, \ldots, m_i$). Note that m_i, the total number of levels (increments) for a given amenity, varies with i, the particular factor under observation. Associated with each level f_{ij} is the cost d_{ij} of effecting the transition from the jth level to the

$(j-1)^{st}$ level on the ith factor. The fact that d_{ij} is allowed to vary for both i (the factor number) and j (the level specification) permits the introduction of nonlinear incremental costs.

Sample tabulations of the level definitions f_{ij} and of the transition costs d_{ij} are shown in Tables 4-1 and 4-2, respectively (pp. 60).

The initial normalized rankings R_i (a set of which are given in Table 5-3, p. 74) are modified to:

$$R_i^* = R_i(j-1) \tag{4.1}$$

where $(j-1)$ = the measure of the distance from comfort, in incremental steps. The number of steps is set by range and meaningful increments.

R_i^* now incorporates the previous knowledge of *patron opinion* (as reflected by the original rankings R_i) and the *need for improvement* at any given station, as reflected by the standing of the station under examination on the table of relative increments. This permits the worst condition to get attention first.

Where R_i was a dimensionless index number, R_i^* is now a modified *number of levels*. This listing of number of levels is to be modified further by *cost*. If cost is used as a *multiplier*, the greater the cost the greater the utility factor, which is counter to the basic point of cost-utility application. If cost is used in *addition* or is *subtracted*, the varying amounts of the costs will destroy the characteristics of the index number because of the inconsistency of the units involved for each amenity and the uncertainties of scale. Scaling, in fact, would become difficult because of a need for unavailable data. Calibration, due to the lack of homogeneity in scale, would be questionable.

Cost, of course, could also be included as a *percentage*; in this case, however, it should be noted that cost in its *absolute form* is valuable to modification of the index number, and there are no data to support such a decision involving percentages.

Finally, the elements of the utility factor might possibly be raised to appropriate powers, in the form

$$\frac{R_i^\alpha}{d_{ij}^\beta}(j-1)^\gamma \tag{4.2}$$

but there is no apparent justification for such a formulation.

The only means, then, by which the index number can retain its character, and at the same time reflect cost-utility (by producing a larger number for a lesser cost) is by its inclusion in the *denominator*:

$$\mu_{ij} = R^*\left(\frac{1}{d_{ij}}\right) \tag{4.3}$$

where $\dfrac{1}{d_{ij}}$ is the inverse of the cost of transition in arriving at comfort level.

This can also be written

$$\mu_{ij} = (\frac{R_i}{d_{ij}})(j-1) \tag{4.4}$$

The utility factor μ_{ij} is seen to incorporate the three aspects described above: *Patron preference, current condition* (state) of an amenity, and *cost of improvement*, weighting more heavily those factors for which a dollar is more productive. The number of increments which will be made will be determined, then, by:

a. The priority of factor i;

b. The *degree of necessity* or distance, in increments, from comfort level, exhibited by the station under inspection;

c. The cost-effectiveness of improving factor i; and

d. The total amount of money available for allocation.

Aspects a, b, and c above are reflected in μ_{ij}. If a predetermined amount of money, A, is provided, to be invested in a particular transit station, the appropriate μ_{ij} values will describe how many units of each amenity need to be improved.

Station weight = S_i

$$\mu_{ij} = S_i (\frac{R_i}{d_{ij}})(j-1) \tag{4.5}$$

Tables can be constructed for ease of identification and manipulation of data. The first table (Table 4-1) should relate specific amenities, and levels of improvement of those amenities, in terms meaningful to the amenities.

Another table (Table 4-2) can be created to show the cost d_{ij} of transition from one level of amenity condition to another.

Note that Table 4-1 illustrates the definition of the distinct, recognizable levels that *can* exist. Table 4-2 illustrates the associated transition costs. In a particular application, the station in question *need not* be at the poorest level for all (or any) amenities. Thus the m_{ij}, the total number of levels (increments) for a given amenity, need not be the value of the poorest level, but simply the existing *initial* level at the time the evaluation is done.

Two methods of employing the utility function developed (Equation 4.4) will be discussed. In the first, a utility function (a variation of μ_{ij} of Equation 4.4) is

Table 4-1
Level Definitions f_{ij} for Various Amenities

Amenity	Level of Improvement⟶
i ↓	Definitions

Table 4-2
Costs d_{ij} for Transition from Level j to Level $j-1$, Amenity i

Amenity	Level of Improvement⟶
i ↓	Costs

computed which results in a recommended *number of increments to be improved for each amenity*. The cost of improving *those* increments is summed and a total is arrived at. By repetition of the method, the budgeted funding amount is approached. In the second method, each utility factor μ_{ij} is considered in turn, and the least costly is accepted until the summation approaches the budgeted amount.

Methodology 1

The *average transition cost D_i* is computed from Table 4-2:

$$D_i = \frac{1}{(m_i - 1)} \sum_{j=2}^{m_i} d_{ij} \tag{4.6}$$

considering only the transitions from *initial* to *ideal* levels. A variant of a utility function, denoted R_i^{**}, is then computed

$$R^{**} = \left(\frac{R_i}{D_i}\right)(m_i - 1) \qquad (4.7)$$

Note that R_i^{**} is not a function of j, and is a column rather than an array of values.

These functions are then normalized to form a utility value w_i:

$$w_i = \frac{R_i^{**}}{AVG(R_i^{**})} = \frac{R_i^{**}}{\frac{1}{n}\sum\limits_{i=1}^{n}R_i^{**}} \qquad (4.8)$$

The following rule is then applied:

1. Values W_i are produced by rounding the w_i to the nearest integer. Should any W_i exceed the number of transitions to Level 1 (i.e., exceed $m_i - 1$); that W_i should be reduced to the lower number.

2. The total cost of moving the amenities W_i levels should be computed from the d_{ij} (i.e., Table 4-2).

3. If the cost computed is less than the resources budgeted, Step 1 should be repeated using $2w_i$ rather than w_i. This procedure should be continued with $3w_i$, $4w_i$, ... until the budgeted funds are as completely utilized as possible.

4. The last set of W_i produced in Step 3 without violating the budget are the recommended set of improvements.

The reduction in W_i in Step 1 is done since it would be meaningless to recommend improvements above the ideal Level 1.

Methodology 2

The set of existing levels are considered. Funds are allocated to that amenity i whose utility factor μ_{ij} is maximum for the transition from the *existing* to the *next* level. This procedure is repeated continually until all budgeted funds are allocated. At each step, "existing level" is interpreted as the most recent one recommended for each amenity. Of course, if any amenities are initially at the ideal level (Level 1), they are not considered as one of the n amenities in either methodology.

5 Test Values: Patron Opinion

Following the order presented in Chapter 4, a *public opinion preference ranking* must be developed. For purposes of example, and to develop "a scale of values based upon user preferences," a survey was devised to extract information representative of the New York City rapid transit system.[1]

In attempting to generalize about the New York City system, with its extremes of both service and amenities, it was felt that, by extension, generalizations could then be made about other systems. The New York City system covers 726 miles of track, which pass through every conceivable economic and ethnic neighborhood type, and is used by every class of society.

The Survey Method

In choosing the mail-back questionnaire form for a system-wide survey of patron opinion of environmental factors in the New York City rapid transit (subway) system, previous experience with this method was considered. It has been found, for instance, that while cost is a drawback to the use of surveys for transportation planning, the mail questionnaire is the cheapest form.[2] In addition, an effective survey is usually brief, and challenges the respondent. Pilot studies are needed to streamline and test feasible questionnaires. Careful survey planning usually delivers a maximum return for the money and time resources available.[3,4] With these strictures in mind, a system-wide mail-back survey was planned.

Questions about procedure concerned the proper arrangement and phrasing of questions, the amount of information which could be expected to be garnered, and the precise definition of "amenities." For this reason, preliminary surveys to test some of these problems were devised.

Preliminary Surveys

Eighteen different questionnaires were designed. Each sought the opinion of the subway user about the quality of one or more of the following features of subway stations:

air conditioning (or temperature)
dust in the air

station cleanliness
noise levels
lighting levels
general appearance
escalator service
directional signs
washroom facilities
seating facilities

It was decided to test various formats of questionnaires at a small number of stations (reducing the total number of variables). The following types of cards were tested:

1. Cards on which the patron had to *rate* the amenities in order of importance to him;
2. Cards on which he had to *choose* a single favored amenity;
3. Cards where a *single amenity* was rated;
4. Cards where a *number of amenities* were rated; and
5. Cards where the patron was asked to fill in his own opinions.

There was some variation in the number of variables (amenities) included on each card. Generally, *temperature* (or *air conditioning*), *dust* in the air, *cleanliness* of floors and walls, *noise*, *light*, and general *appearance* were used, but some cards mentioned washroom facilities, escalator service, or directional signs in addition.

There was also variation in the rating systems; generally "excellent," "good," "acceptable," "unacceptable," "hazardous," were used, but in some cases "good," "acceptable," and "bad" were employed.

Two sizes of cards were used, since it was expected that many patrons might not pocket the larger (4" X 8-1/2") cards used. This card had the advantage of carrying more information, but it was anticipated that the smaller card (4" X 6") would be more acceptable in rate of return.

Four trains were also selected for the distribution of a related set of questionnaires; the trains were on the E and F routes running from Continental to Roosevelt Avenues in the borough of Queens. The trains investigated were:

R 1 (old);
R 38 (fairly new);
R 40 (not air-conditioned; and
R 40 or R 42 (air-conditioned).

Questionnaire cards were printed in four different colors to designate the four stations (or the four trains) on which the mail-back cards were issued. In addition, white cards were printed to be issued to patrons for completion and immediate return. Comparison of the relative costs of mail-back and immediate-response cards was thereby made possible.

The preliminary surveys required that patrons respond immediately to the questionnaires. The test reflected an attempt to get patron reaction to rating amenities with:

> *no* reference to money;
> reference to "government" money;
> reference to the *patron's* money;
> the *apportionment* of a sum ($1.00) of money.

In the last case, it was initially intended to relate amenity-rating directly to a portion of a *fare* or *fare increase*, but this wording was unacceptable to the New York City Transit Authority because the timing of the survey happened to coincide with an actual fare increase, and changes in the questionnaire format were therefore made.

Four stations of the New York City transit system were selected for the preliminary survey on subway station improvement. They were chosen because they are identical in physical layout, and they offer comparable quality of service to the user while serving substantially different user groups. The subway patrons of these stations can be characterized as, respectively:

> upper and upper-middle class professionals;
> lower economic levels (the disadvantaged and poor);
> lower and middle (clerical) classes; and
> suburban middle class.

This information was obtained from general observation and knowledge of the areas in question.

A total of 7200 cards (of which 1800 were collected on the spot and 5400 were mail return) were distributed.

Summary of Results of Preliminary Surveys

Of those cards which asked the patron to *rate* the amenities, the following order emerged, representing *order of needed improvement*:

1. station cleaning
2. air conditioning (or temperature improvement)
3. dust in the air
4. general appearance

5. noise levels
6. lighting levels
7. need for escalators
8. need for benches

Of those cards which asked the patron to *judge the relative level of a single amenity*, the following was the result: (worst first)

1. dust in the air
2. temperature

with the remaining amenities judged on a par.

Of those cards which asked the patron to *choose the single worst condition* (from a listing), the following was found:

1. washrooms
2. temperature
3. dust, cleaning, appearance
4. noise
5. light
6. escalators

There was a remarkable consistency among the first few choices, whether the cards had a listing of all amenities to be judged, or a single amenity; whether a rating was requested, or a single worst case asked for; whether cards were filled out on the spot, or returned by mail later. The first few were invariably *dust, cleanliness, appearance, temperature,* not necessarily in that order.

General Conclusions from Preliminary Surveys

1. A mail-back card is preferable to a filled-out-in-place card: there is a greater return for a shorter working time in pursuing the survey, and it might be concluded that responses are given more consideration.

2. The card should provide for patron comment on all aspects of the system: either through inclusion as a "ratable," or through the use of a comments box.

3. The card should in some way involve the patron in rating the variables on an *economic* scale.

4. The rating system should be for all variables at one time rather than individually.

5. The rating system must be simple to comprehend.

6. The wording on the card must be comprehensible and as unambiguous as possible.

7. The placement of a given amenity variable first on a survey card might have influenced its popularity in choice; therefore the variables should be arranged randomly on different cards.

8. *Better service* as a category should be added as a base for comparison with amenities.

9. The money rating system should be related as closely as possible to cost per ride in order to present patrons with as realistic a choice as possible.

Qualitative Discussion of the Results of Preliminary Surveys

The following analysis is based upon a detailed examination of the results of the preliminary surveys.

1. *Air conditioning* and *cleanliness* were the areas most consistently identified for improvement. In addition, those surveyed expressed a strong interest in better *washroom facilities*, when this question was posed, while all other items were lumped together in the middle of the ratings in a manner which indicates no strong discrimination by the public.

2. Mailed-back responses were either less critical than, or the same as, those filled out in the station. This perhaps represents more thought and reflection on the part of the respondent (this deduction is based on the shifts noted, in particular from *hazardous* to *unacceptable* in response to questions dealing with, for example, *noise*).

3. People are motivated to respond to a questionnaire concerning subways. The total average response rate in the mailed-back part of the survey had results averaging better than 20 percent. In one instance there was a 40 percent response rate.

4. People expressed a desire to answer a *number* of questions. The ultimate questionnaire must provide the rider with the opportunity for a mild catharsis in a number of areas. From public reaction, it can be concluded that single-feature questionnaires are not effective from a public relations point of view.

5. Responses to questions phrased in a negative fashion were not answered in what appears to be a realistic way. *Light* levels in the subway are not "hazardous" by most usual criteria. Yet a significant number of people said so, effectively saying "bad" but without any thought as to the meaning of the word "hazardous."

6. No significant deviation was detected in the responses from the different stations. However, the data was insufficient to provide any high degree of confidence in this conclusion.

A Follow-up Survey

At the request of the New York City Transit Authority, the pilot survey requested that patrons indicate their preferences concerning subway improvements without reference to the fare. Upon examination of the results, and in light of the fact that improvements do entail costs, a follow-up survey was conducted to learn whether the response would change if it were made clear that some monetary outlay would be involved.

The results of the follow-up survey were in agreement with those obtained during the first survey. In particular, *temperature control* and *station appearance* placed first and second, respectively.

The inclusion of a *comments* section resulted in many interesting responses. In addition to the improvements listed, patrons indicated their desire for speedier and prompter service, as well as for more police, both of which factors were included in the final survey card.

The System-wide Survey

Based upon the results of the preliminary surveys and the short follow-up survey used to test the response characteristics of the transit-using public, a questionnaire was designed for the system-wide survey incorporating the better design features of the various questionnaires used in the pilot survey. The questionnaire was designed to:

1. Test the reactions of the public to the improvement of ten different features of the subway stations.

2. Require the public to relate the improvement desired to an economic scale.

3. Eliminate extremes in reaction by excluding such words as "hazardous."

4. Allow the people to make any suggestions or criticisms they might wish to make.

Figure 5-1 is the questionnaire used in the system-wide survey.

Twenty-five subway stations were selected at random from the total of 476 stations in the present New York City transit system. Their locations are categorized as follows:

Manhattan	8	Elevated	10
Brooklyn	11	Underground	14
Bronx	2	Open Cut	1
Queens	4		

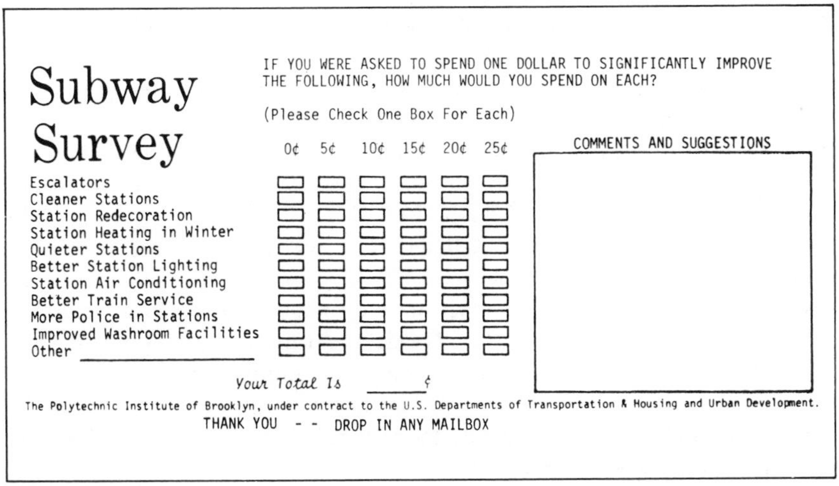

Subway Survey

IF YOU WERE ASKED TO SPEND ONE DOLLAR TO SIGNIFICANTLY IMPROVE THE FOLLOWING, HOW MUCH WOULD YOU SPEND ON EACH?

(Please Check One Box For Each)

0¢ 5¢ 10¢ 15¢ 20¢ 25¢

Escalators
Cleaner Stations
Station Redecoration
Station Heating in Winter
Quieter Stations
Better Station Lighting
Station Air Conditioning
Better Train Service
More Police in Stations
Improved Washroom Facilities
Other __________

COMMENTS AND SUGGESTIONS

Your Total Is ______ ¢

The Polytechnic Institute of Brooklyn, under contract to the U.S. Departments of Transportation & Housing and Urban Development.

THANK YOU - - DROP IN ANY MAILBOX

Figure 5-1. Questionnaire Survey Mail-Back Card.

A list of these stations, by borough, is presented as part of Table 7-2 (p. 96).

Crews of three handed out the cards at locations near turnstiles, token booths, and exit stairs during the afternoon rush hour. The hour selected for each station was chosen as the peak hour for that station, which varied with the station's location in the city.

Results of the Survey

The analysis of variance technique was used to analyze the results of the survey. The responses of those polled were replaced by the *ranks* of those responses, thereby eliminating the bias created by the fact that many of the money allocations did not add up to one dollar.

This technique was first suggested by Milton Friedman[5] (an equivalent procedure called "Concordance Analysis" was suggested by M.G. Kendall[6]).

The method of analysis is also based on two schemes suggested by R.A. Fisher.[7] The first scheme suggests that there is an arithmetic identity which permits the sum of squares of deviations about the mean of pooled samples to be broken into two parts. The first part is the sum of squares of individual subsamples about their own means, and the second part is the sum of squares of the subsample means about the mean of the pooled samples.

The second scheme is Fisher's Randomization Analysis, connected with a specified experiment (see appendix).

Of the approximately 20,000 questionnaires distributed, the responding sample size was 3678, a response rate of 18.4 percent.

A substantial proportion (39.2 percent) of those returned did not add up to $1.00. In these cases the data was normalized (i.e., if $0.50 was the total spent, each response was multiplied by 2; 2 × .50 = $1.00).

A review of the data showed that five of the six responses were most frequently used. Very few people spent 20¢ on anything. It is thought that a person motivated to spend that much on a particular feature when on to the next convenient denomination: 25¢. The data lent itself to a rank test scheme much better than those test schemes which imply a normalcy.

The use of rank values (in place of the measurements themselves) for the purpose of significant tests simplified the analysis very considerably.[8] The rank values in each grouping are summarized, and these "rank-sums" then used in the Analysis of Variance procedure.

From a general review of the results it is apparent that people cared much less about *better washrooms* and *more police* than they cared about *cleaner, better decorated* and *heated* stations. The question of *better train service* had an almost 0, 1 distribution: people either spending nothing, or 25¢.

The first choice for improvement, by station, is given in Table 5-1, which shows the general consistency of response for cleaner stations. The overall result is as shown in Table 5-2 by order of rank-sums. If rank-sums are normalized (as in column 4 of Table 5-2) a rating is achieved. Gross expenditure can also be used to rank, or rate, the amenities. The same Table 5-2 shows the minor changes produced by use of this variable. Of course, eliminating the "other" classification produces the ranking and rating seen in Table 5-3.

The use to which patron desires are to be put must determine the form of ranking or rating. Since this survey was intended to form the basis of a resource allocation index, normalized gross expenditures were used.[9]

Further analysis was directed at considering the possibility of whether patrons rated the *specific station at which cards were handed out*, or the *entire system*. Results were therefore broken down by various known conditions, and subjected to analysis of variance testing. Testing by individual stations by underground vs. elevated station, by level of income of the surrounding population, by borough, by type of lighting (incandescent or fluorescent), and by number of levels, was done to find if known variables at the various stations influenced choices. The results showed that, with remarkable consistency, patrons rated the *system*. Figures 5-2 through 5-6 show the lack of correlation between station conditions and patron responses, by station, for some of the variables tested, using either mean expenditure or rank of an amenity tested.

Table 5-1
Primary Choice for Improvement by Station

Station Number	Amenity Rated First			
	Cleaner Stations	Escalators	Station Heating	Redecoration
1	X			
2	X			
3	X			
4		X		
5	X			
6	X			
7	X			
8	X			
9		X		
10			X	
11	X			
12	X			
13	X			
14	X			
15			X	
16	X			
17	X			
18	X			
19				X
20	X			
21	X			
22		X		
23	X			
24	X			
25	X			

Table 5-2
Amenities by Rank-Sum and Gross Expenditure

Amenity	Rank-Sum	Normalized	Rank by Rank Sum	Gross Expenditure	Normalized	Rank by Gross Expenditure
Station cleaning	28731.00	.118	1	60,042	.165	1
Station heating	25887.50	.107	2	46,178	.127	3
Station redecoration	24745.50	.102	3	44,707	.123	4
Escalators	24184.50	.100	4	52,129	.144	2
Better train service	23801.50	.098	5	38,405	.136	5
Station lighting	22616.00	.093	6	28,568	.079	7
Quieter stations	21680.00	.089	7	29,023	.080	6
More police	20173.00	.083	8	23,351	.064	8
Air conditioning	20035.50	.083	9	21,741	.060	9
Improved washrooms	15963.50	.066	10	10,117	.028	10
Other	14666.00	.061	11	8,892	.024	11

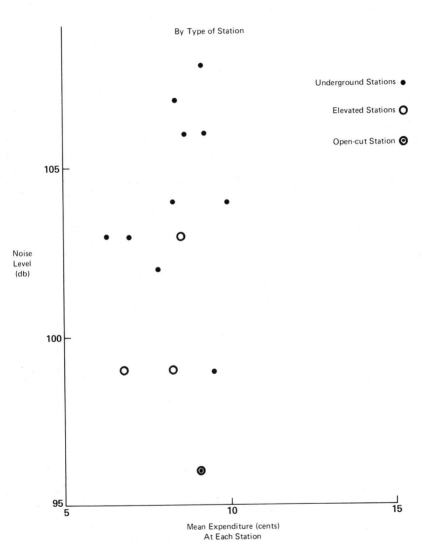

Figure 5-2. Noise Level vs. Expenditure by Public.

Table 5-3
Final Rankings and Ratings

Amenity	Normalized Rank Sum	Rank	Normalized Gross Expenditure	Rank
Cleaning	.126	1	.169	1
Heating	.114	2	.130	3
Redecoration	.109	3	.126	4
Escalator	.106	4	.147	2
Train service	.104	5	.108	5
Lighting	.099	6	.081	7
Noise	.095	7	.082	6
Police	.089	8	.066	8
Air conditioning	.088	9	.061	9
Washrooms	.070	10	.029	10

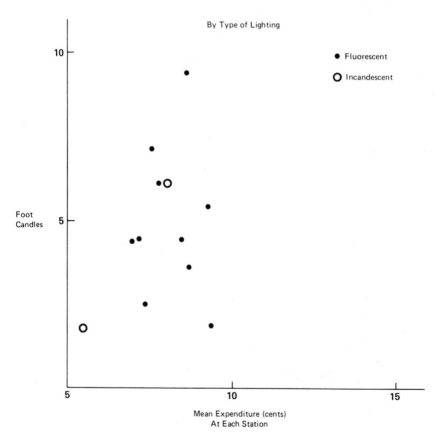

Figure 5-3. Light Level vs. Expenditure by Public.

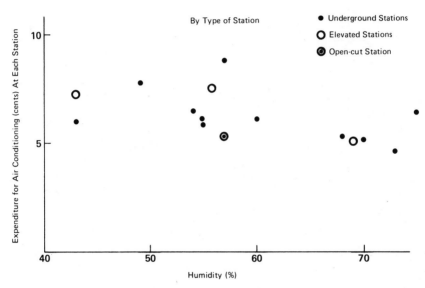

Figure 5-4. Humidity vs. Expenditure by Public.

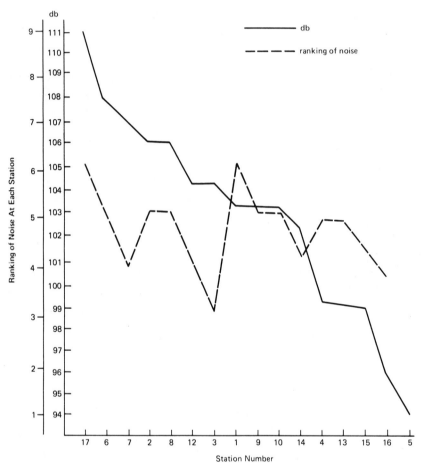

Figure 5-5. Noise Level of Stations vs. Ranking of Noise.

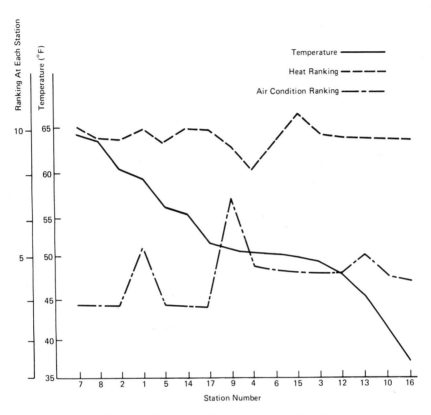

Figure 5-6. Station Temperatures vs. Ranking.

6 Test Values: Acceptable
Comfort Levels

Summary of Factors Used

Continuing the order presented in Chapter 4, *a set of average comfort or acceptance levels* of the amenities rated and ranked by the public must be developed. To summarize the factors to be used in this application of the methodology:

Convenience

Escalators will be limited (for purposes of ease of manipulation in this study) to the installation of 2-foot-wide, 25-foot-rise units.

Better train service will be represented by the addition of trains to peak or off-peak service for the reduction of headway, or waiting time.

Washroom adequacy is limited to the maintenance, in a safe, sanitary condition, of existing washrooms, not consideration of the need for installation of new units (which could, however, be brought into the methodology).

Cleanliness

While air pollution was measured as a yardstick of cleanliness, the measure to be used in this book will be the more apparent one (to the riding public) of floor and wall cleanliness (general appearance having proven of great importance in the rankings). This choice also permits greater ease of calculation of costs per incremental improvement, for purposes of transportation.

Aesthetics or Redecoration

Aesthetics in a subway station could be improved by a number of means:

1. *Painting.* The New York City Transit Authority has a repainting schedule of 10 years.[1] Painting is the minimum which can be done to improve the appearance of a station, and it could be done on a 5-, 10-, or 15-year basis.

2. *Furniture.* New, modern benches, railings, stairway appurtenances, refuse cans, column covers, and signing could be used to replace existing furniture and improve overall appearance.

3. *Walls* have been tiled since the beginning of rapid transit systems, for the

sole purpose of permitting ease of cleaning and providing a certain degree of resistance to breaking and vandalism. Both these qualities can be provided with a number of modern materials, such as other forms of tile, aluminum, stainless steel, epoxy compounds. Such materials would permit the introduction of some individuality into station decor to replace the existing sameness.

4. *Floors* also retain their original concrete ostensibly for the same reasons as walls retain their tile. Yet modern materials can be used to provide ease of cleaning, nonslip surface, and durability, while providing some introduction of color and design.

5. *Ceilings.* The vaulted ceilings of the stations are painted once in 10 years under current scheduling. Suspended ceilings can certainly be installed which would still permit movement of air as needed yet provide pleasant aspects of light and appearance and sound absorption.

Temperature

1. *Heating.* The importance of maintaining reasonable temperatures is apparent from the literature. The subway patron has no personal means of warming himself, is relatively motionless on station platforms, and can become extremely, even dangerously, cold at times. The assumption of "average waiting time" is an unrealistic deception. Waiting times during peak hours are on the order of 1 or 2 minutes; during off-peak hours they can approach an hour or more. The "average," therefore, is insufficient in assessing discomfort.

2. *Cooling.* Air conditioning the subway car was considered impossible a few years ago. Now it is the station which is "impractical" to cool except through the use of fans.[2] Means can certainly be found to cool subway stations or portions thereof. From the earlier material, 5-degree increments have been taken as significant, between the limits (Tables 3-5 and 3-6, and Figures 3-1, 3-2, 3-5 and 3-6) of 40 and 105 degrees.

Noise

It is apparent that this "amenity" is a quality of transportation systems which has been most greatly ignored and shunted aside. Noise "can kill," as was quoted earlier, and before it finally kills it can affect the human organism in varying degrees, temporarily and permanently, to the point at which, short of death, it "can drive you crazy."[3]

For the purpose of this allocation index, 85 db is taken as "comfort level," even though it has been found that 80 or 90 db can contribute to accidents, dilate the pupils, and cause the skin to pale and the flow of adrenalin to increase. Such physical changes caused by noise may be enough to impair efficiency and coordination and thereby cause accidents, by causing a person suddenly to focus away from his tasks.[4] Three-decibel increments are taken as significant.

Illumination

Fifteen foot-candles are set as "comfort" level, with decrements based on Tables 3-17 and 3-18.

Safety and Security

Safety and security, in this book, are described in terms of stationed policemen, as the most easily perceived element of safety from the patron's point of view.

Establishment of Meaningful Increments

Cleaning

"Comfort" level for cleaning stations is taken as one man on duty at all times, whether cleaning floors or walls for an average station of 20,000 SF floor area. *Noticeable increments* are established at:

Level 1:	3 shifts/day	(24 man-hour/day)
Level 2:	2 shifts/day	(16 man-hour/day)
Level 3:	1 shift/day	(8 man-hour/day)
Level 4:	1/2 shift/day	(4 man-hour/day)
Level 5:	1/4 shift/day	(2 man-hour/day)
Level 6:	1/8 shift/day	(1 man-hour/day)

Escalators

Comfort level is set at one 48-inch-wide escalator to the surface per 6000 persons/peak hour in increments of 25-foot rise.[5]
  Noticeable increments are established at:

Level 1: to surface
Level 2: to 25' below surface
Level 3: to 50' below surface
Level 4: to 75' below surface
Level 5: to 100' below surface
Level 6: to 125' below surface
Level 7: to 150' below surface
Level 8: to 175' below surface

Let 40 percent of capacity be required to go to the next step (6000 persons/peak hour = 1 escalator, 8400 persons/peak hour = 2 escalators, etc.).

Heating

Comfort level is set at 72° F, with increments of 5° F.
Noticeable increments are established at:

Level 1: 72° F
Level 2: 67° F
Level 3: 62° F
Level 4: 57° F
Level 5: 52° F
Level 6: 47° F
Level 7: 42° F

Redecoration

Comfort level is set at complete redecoration, including painting, new furniture, new ceilings, new walls, new floors.
Noticeable increments are established at:

Level 1: new ceilings
Level 2: new walls
Level 3: new floors
Level 4: new furniture
Level 5: painting every 5 years
Level 6: painting every 10 years
Level 7: painting every 15 years

Train Service

Comfort level is set at 1 1/2-minute headways during peak hours; 10-minute headways during off-peak operation.
Noticeable increments are established at:

1. Peak Hour Operation (2 hours/day)
   Level 1: 1 1/2-minute headway = 40 trains/hour
   Level 2: 2 1/2-minute headway = 24 trains/hour
   Level 3: 4-minute headway   = 15 trains/hour
   Level 4: 6-minute headway   = 10 trains/hour
   Level 5: 9-minute headway   = 7 trains/hour

2. Off-Peak Hour Operation (22 hours/day)
Level 1: 10-minute headway   = 6 trains/hour
Level 2: 15-minute headway   = 4 trains/hour
Level 3: 20-minute headway   = 3 trains/hour
Level 4: 30-minute headway   = 2 trains/hour
Level 5: 45-minute headway   = 1 train/hour

Noise Control

Comfort level is set at a complete noise suppression program, including automatic rail lubricators; rail with resilient fasteners; track on floating slab; rail grinding; and acoustical treatment of station.
Noticeable increments are established at:

Level 1: acoustical treatment of station (ceiling and walls)
Level 2: rail grinding
Level 3: track on floating slab
Level 4: rail with resilient fasteners
Level 5: automatic rail lubricators
Level 6: no treatment

The assumption is made that each treatment reduces noise by 3 db.

Illumination

Comfort level is set at 15 foot-candles.
Noticeable increments are established at:

Level 1: 15 foot-candles
Level 2: 10 foot-candles
Level 3: 5 foot-candles
Level 4: 2 foot-candles
Level 5: 1.2 foot-candles

Police

Comfort level is set at one 24-hour post/20,000 square feet.
Noticeable increments are established at:

Level 1: one 24-hour post/20,000 square feet
Level 2: one 16-hour post/20,000 square feet
Level 3: one 8-hour post/20,000 square feet
Level 4: one 4-hour post/20,000 square feet
Level 5: one 1-hour post/20,000 square feet

Air Conditioning

Comfort level is set at 72° F.
   Noticeable increments are established at 5° F.

     Level 1:   72° F
     Level 2:   77° F
     Level 3:   82° F
     Level 4:   87° F
     Level 5:   92° F
     Level 6:   97° F
     Level 7: 102° F

Washroom Facilities

Comfort level is set at 8 man-hours/day maintenance, plus 4 man-hours/day police.
   Noticeable increments are established at:

     Level 1:   8 MH/D maintenance +   4 MH/D police
     Level 2:   4 MH/D maintenance +   2 MH/D police
     Level 3:   2 MH/D maintenance +   1 MH/D police
     Level 4:   1 MH/D maintenance + 1/2 MH/D police
     Level 5: 1/2 MH/D maintenance +   0 MH/D police
     Level 6: 1/4 MH/D maintenance +   0 MH/D police

   Table 6-1 summarizes the preceding development of increments.

Table 6-1
Establishment of Noticeable Environmental Incremental Levels

Amenity	Level 10	Level 9	Level 8	Level 7	Level 6	Level 5	Level 4	Level 3	Level 2	(comfort) Level 1
1. Cleaning stations (shifts/day)						1/4	1/2	1	2	3
2. Escalators (feet below surface)			175	150	125	100	75	50	25	0
3. Heating (degrees F)	27	32	37	42	47	52	57	62	67	72
4. Redecoration (type)				Paint 15-yr	Paint 10-yr	Paint 5-yr	Furniture	Floor	Walls	Ceilings
5. Peak hour train service (headway in minutes)						9	6	4	2-1/2	1-1/2
6. Off-peak train service (headway in minutes)						45	30	20	15	10
7. Noise control ([db]/type)					[100+] No treatment	Automatic [97] rail lubricators	Rail [94] with resilient fasteners	Track [91] on floating slab	Rail [88] grinding	[85] Acoustical treatment
8. Lighting (foot-candles)						1.2	2	5	10	15
9. Police coverage (man-hrs/day)						2	4	8	16	24
10. Air conditioning (degrees F)				102	97	92	87	82	77	72
11. Washrooms (total man-hrs/day)					1/4	1/2	1-1/2	3	6	12

7

**Test Values:
Improvement Cost**

Unit Cost of Improvement

Completing the order presented in Chapter 4, a *unit cost of improvement* is finally required.

In the present example real values are required for:

1. Cleaning
2. Escalators
3. Station heating
4. Redecoration
5. Train service
6. Noise reduction
7. Station lighting
8. Safety (police; protection)
9. Station cooling; air conditioning
10. Washroom maintenance and policing

Cleaning

Salary of one man is estimated at $5000 ± per year; therefore, total cost is estimated (per man) at $9688 ± with overhead, or $29,063/year for 24 man-hours per day.

Level 1: comfort level @ 3 man-years/year cost @ $29,063/year for average station of 20,000 square feet
Level 2: 16 MH/D = 2 MY/Y = $14,063/yr/20,000 SF
Level 3: 8 MH/D = 1 MY/Y = 6,563/yr/20,000 SF
Level 4: 4 MH/D = 1/2 MY/Y = 2,813/yr/20,000 SF
Level 5: 2 MH/D = 1/4 MY/Y = 938/yr/20,000 SF
Level 6: no service = 0

Then the cost per increment is:

from Level 6 to 5 = $ 938/yr = Step 5
Level 5 to 4 = 1,875/yr = Step 4
Level 4 to 3 = 3,750/yr = Step 3

Level 3 to 2 = 7,500/yr = Step 2
Level 2 to 1 = 15,000/yr = Step 1

Overload: Since the basic measure of this amenity is a 20,000-square-foot station, the next level of cleaning is taken at *10 percent*, or 20,000 square feet, to justify another unit of cleaning.

Escalators

The New York City Transit Authority has estimated an average cost of an installation as from $300,000 to $350,000, and up to $1 million in some cases, plus $11,400 per year for maintenance.[1]

Say cost per unit (one 25-foot-rise escalator) = $200,000 @ 20 years = $10,000/year (including maintenance).

Step 1: $10,000/6000 persons peak hour
Step 2: $10,000/6000 persons peak hour
Step 3: $10,000/6000 persons peak hour
Step 4: $10,000/6000 persons peak hour
Step 5: $10,000/6000 persons peak hour
Step 6: $10,000/6000 persons peak hour
Step 7: $10,000/6000 persons peak hour

Overload: Since the basic measure of this amenity is 6000 persons per hour to justify one escalator, the next level of *Escalator* is taken at *40 percent*, or 2400 persons per hour, to justify another escalator.

Heating

For elevated stations, the Transit Authority has estimated $500/location/year for electric power for existing heaters, and $150 per new heater.[2] This represents, if we assume 2000 square feet/installation, a cost of $0.32/cubic foot.

Another source provides a figure of $0.40 per cubic foot.[3] For ten increments of 5° rise each, each increment will be $0.04/cubic foot:

Step 1 = $0.04/CF/year
Step 2 = $0.04/CF/year
Step 3 = $0.04/CF/year
Step 4 = $0.04/CF/year
Step 5 = $0.04/CF/year
Step 6 = $0.04/CF/year
Step 7 = $0.04/CF/year

Redecoration

The New York City Transit Authority spends $0.15/square foot for painting stations, estimating $15,000 for the average station.[4]

From another source, the average cost for wall treatments such as:

    acrylic or epoxy
    exposed aggregate/epoxy
    vinyl plastic
    urethane
    copper sheets
    wood veneer
    wallguard

may be summarized at $2.20/square foot; divided by 20 years = $0.11/square foot/year.[5]

    Floors: $2.50/SF ÷ 20 yrs = $0.13/SF/yr.
    Ceilings: (Suspended) $2.50/SF ÷ 10 yrs = $0.25/SF/yr.

New furniture should be replaced in 15 years; cost may be estimated at $5,000; annual cost = $350 per 20,000/SF (average station).

Painting @ $0.15/SF

for 5 years	=	.03/SF/yr
for 10 years	=	.015/SF/yr
for 15 years	=	.01/SF/yr

Then increments for redecoration are:

Step 1	=	$0.25/SF/yr
Step 2	=	$0.11/SF/yr
Step 3	=	$0.13/SF/yr
Step 4	=	$350.00/20,000/SF/yr
Step 5	=	$0.015/SF/yr
Step 6	=	0.005/SF/yr
Step 7	=	0.01/SF/yr

Peak Hour Train Service

Assuming equipment is already available:
    1 motorman and 1 conductor/train @ $20,000/yr (including overhead)

10 cars/train
15¢/car-mile electricity cost
15 miles average run
5 days/week = 250 days/year
2 peak hours
22 off-peak hours
$2.00/car-hour of service maintenance cost

Then for

Step 4   add 6 men @ 20,000 = 120,000/yr
add 30 cars × 15 miles × 0.15/car-mi × 2 hrs × 250 days

$$\underbrace{\phantom{\text{add 30 cars} \times 15 \text{ miles} \times 0.15/\text{car-mi} \times 2 \text{ hrs} \times 250 \text{ days}}}_{1125.0}$$

= $33,750/yr
add 30 cars × 2 hours × 250 days × $2.00/car-hr of service

$$\underbrace{\phantom{\text{add 30 cars} \times 2 \text{ hours} \times 250 \text{ days} \times \$2.00/\text{car-hr of service}}}_{1000.0}$$

= $30,000/yr
Total   = $183,750/yr   (say 185,000)

Step 3   add 10 men @ 20,000   = 200,000/yr
add 50 cars × 1125.0   = $56,250
add 50 cars × 1000.0   = $ 50,000

    Total $306,250 (say 300,000)

Step 2   add 18 men @ 20,000 = 360,000/yr
add 90 cars × 1125.0 = 101,250
add 90 cars × 1000.0 =   90,000

    Total $551,250 (say 550,000)

Step 1   add 32 men @ 20,000   = 640,000/yr
add 160 cars × 1125.0   = 180,000
add 160 cars × 1000.0   = 160,000

    Total $980,000/yr (say 980,000)

For an average 15-mile run,

Step 4 = $185,000 ÷ 15 = $12,333/mile/year
Step 3 = $300,000 ÷ 15 = $20,000/mile/year
Step 2 = $550,000 ÷ 15 = $36,666/mile/year
Step 1 = $980,000 ÷ 15 = $65,333/mile/year

Overload: Since the basic measure of this amenity is one mile of route, next level of train service is taken at *50 percent*, or one-half mile, to justify another unit of train service.

Off-peak Train Service

For

Step 4   add 2 men @ 20,000 = 40,000/yr

add 10 cars × 15 miles × $.15/car-mile × 22 hrs × 250 days

$$\underbrace{}$$

12,375.0

= $123,750

add 10 cars × 22 hrs × 250 days × $2.00/car-hr

$$\underbrace{}$$

10,997.7

= $109,980

Total   = $273,730/yr   (say 275,000)

Step 3   = $273,730/yr   (say 275,000)

Step 2   = $273,730/yr   (say 275,000)

Step 1   add 4 men   = $ 80,000/yr

          add 20 cars   = $247,500

          add 20 cars   = $219,960

          Total   = $547,460   (say 550,000)

Then for an average 15-mile run,

Step 4 = $275,000 ÷ 15 = $18,333/mile/year
Step 3 = $275,000 ÷ 15 = $18,333/mile/year
Step 2 = $275,000 ÷ 15 = $18,333/mile/year
Step 1 = $550,000 ÷ 15 = $36,666/mile/year

Overload: Since the basic measure of this amenity is one mile of route, next level of train service is taken at *50 percent*, or one-half mile, to justify another unit of train service.

Noise

The New York City Transit Authority estimates the following costs for various means of attenuating noise production:

Trackwork

Rail grinding: four miles/night @ $800.
Automatic rail lubricators: $15,000/location.
Rail with resilient fasteners cost 1.5 times conventional rail: $800,000/track-mile (= $150/foot) versus $530,000 per track-mile (= $100/foot).
Track on "floating slab": $300/foot.
The total cost to treat an underground station is estimated at $100,000.
Acoustic material on tunnel walls: $150/square foot.
Acoustic material in fan and vent ducts: $1.25/square foot.[6]

Then on an incremental, unit basis:

Rail grinding costs $800 for 4 miles = 800 ÷ 20,000 = $0.04/ft. of rail × 2 rails per track = $0.08/ft. of track/year (to be done annually).
Automatic rail lubricators @ $15,000/location should last 10 years:[7] $1500/yr. (assume one location per station).
Replacing rail with *resilient fasteners* costs $150/foot of track,[8] if it lasts 15 years, 150 ÷ 15 = $10.00/ft. of track/year.
Acoustical treatment of a station @ $100,000;[9] say it lasts 15 years = $6500/yr. (walls) ÷ 20,000 SF = .32/SF/yr.
Track on "floating slab" @ $300/ft. of track;[10] if it lasts 15 years, 300 ÷ 15 = $20,000/ft. of track/year.

To summarize:

Step 1 = $ 20.00/ft of track/year
Step 2 = $ 0.32/SF of walls and ceilings/year
Step 3 = $ 10.00/ft of track/year
Step 4 = $1500.00/track/year
Step 5 = $ 0.08/ft of track/year

Illumination

At $75 each fluorescent fixture; in a 20,000 SF station, say 10 fixtures @ $75 = $750 will raise the lighting level one foot-candle = 750/20,000 = .04/SF/fc including cost of power and maintenance.

Step 1 = $0.20/SF/yr.
Step 2 = $ .20/SF/yr.
Step 3 = $ .12/SF/yr.
Step 4 = $ .04/SF/yr.

Police Protection

The cost to cover a post for a 24-hour period (4.2 Patrolmen) is $195.17.[11]
  Therefore the annual cost = 365 × 195.17 = $71,237.05; say $71,250 per 20,000 square feet.

  Then 16-hour coverage = $47,500/20,000 SF/yr.
        8-hour coverage = $23,750/20,000 SF/yr.
        4-hour coverage = $11,875/20,000 SF/yr.
        2-hour coverage = $ 5,938/20,000 SF/yr.
        1-hour coverage = $ 2,969/200,000 SF/yr.

Overload: Since the basic measure of this amenity is a 20,000-square-foot station, the next level of police service is taken at *60 percent*, or 12,000 square feet, to justify another unit of police service.

Air Conditioning

At a cost of $1875/ton,[12] say 20 tons/100,000/CF/5° F = 1875 × 20 = $37,500/100,000 CF/5° F = $.38/CF/5° F. Then each increment (10 increments) = $0.038/CF.

      Step 1 = $0.038/CF/yr.
      Step 2 = $0.038/CF/yr.
      Step 3 = $0.038/CF/yr.
      Step 4 = $0.038/CF/yr.
      Step 5 = $0.038/CF/yr.
      Step 6 = $0.038/CF/yr.

Washrooms

The cost to equip a toilet-washroom is given as $18,500.[13] The cost to install a complete washroom-toilet is $50,000.
  Maintenance cost is $90.00 per week or $9,531/yr. (with overhead).
  Police cost is $195.17/24-hr. post.

  Then

      8 man-hrs. maintenance/day costs $9531/yr./20,000 SF/yr.
      4 man-hrs. maintenance/day costs $4610/yr./20,000 SF/yr.
      2 man-hrs. maintenance/day costs $1562/yr./20,000 SF/yr.

1 man-hr. maintenance/day costs $ 625/yr./20,000 SF/yr.
1/2 man-hr. maintenance/day costs $ 312/yr./20,000 SF/yr.
1/4 man-hr. maintenance/day costs $ 156/yr./20,000 SF/yr.
Police cost is @ $195.17/24-hr. post.

Then

4 man-hrs./day police coverage = $11,875/20,000 SF/yr.
2 man-hrs./day police coverage = $ 5,938/20,000 SF/yr.
1 man-hr. /day police coverage = $ 2,969/20,000 SF/yr.
1/2 man-hr. /day police coverage = $ 1,485/20,000 SF/yr.

Total cost at each level	= $9531 + 11,875	= $21,406 (Level 1)
	= 4610 + 5938	= 10,548 (Level 2)
	= 1562 + 2969	= 4531 (Level 3)
	= 625 + 1485	= 2110 (Level 4)
	= 312	= 312 (Level 5)
	= 156	= 156 (Level 6)

Then

Step 1 = $10,858
Step 2 = $ 6017
Step 3 = $ 2421
Step 4 = $ 1798
Step 5 = $ 156
Step 6 = $ 156

Overload: Since the basic increment is a 20,000-square-foot station, the next level of washroom service is taken at *60 percent*, or 2000 square feet, to justify another unit of washroom service.

Table 7-1 is presented next as a visual summary of the units, incremental weights, and costs used for each environmental factor.

Concurrent Ambient Conditions
Measurement Survey

At the same time as the patron opinion survey was being made, the ambient levels of *light, temperature, relative humidity, air pollution,* and *noise* were measured in the same stations. This was done to be able to test the question of whether patrons would rate the *individual station* at which they received the questionnaire, or the *system* (or that portion of the system with which they were familiar) *as a whole*.

Table 7-1
Cost in Dollars d_{ij} for Transition Step from Level j to Level $(j-1)$, Amenity i

Amenity i	10	9	8	7	6	5	4	3	2	1 (Comfort)	Dimensions & Units
1. Cleaning stations						938 (X_1)	1,875 (X_1)	3,750 (X_1)	7,500 (X_1)	15,000 (X_1)	X_1 = SF* of Floor; 20,000 SF unit
2. Escalators			10,000 (X_7)	10,000 (X_7)	10,000 (X_7)	10,000 (X_7)	10,000 (X_7)	10,000 (X_7)	10,000 (X_7)	10,000 (X_7)	X_7 = peak hour volume (persons); 6,000 persons unit
3. Heating	0.04 (X_3)	0.04 (X_3)	0.04 (X_3)	0.04 (X_3)	0.04 (X_3)	0.04 (X_3)	0.04 (X_3)	0.04 (X_3)	0.04 (X_3)	0.04 (X_3)	X_3 = CF** of Station Volume; 1 CF unit
4. Redecoration				0.01 (X_4)	0.005 (X_4)	0.015 (X_4)	350 (X_1)	0.13 (X_1)	0.11 (X_5)	0.25 (X_4)	X_1 = SF of Floor; 1 SF Unit; X_4 = SF of Ceiling; 1 SF Unit; X_5 = SF of Wall; 1 SF Unit
5. Peak hour train service						12,333 (X_6)	20,000 (X_6)	36,666 (X_6)	36,666 (X_6)	65,333 (X_6)	X_6 = miles of train run; 1 mile unit
6. Off-peak train service						18,333 (X_6)	18,333 (X_6)	18,333 (X_6)	18,333 (X_6)	36,666 (X_6)	X_6 = miles of train run; 1 mile unit
7. Noise control					0.08 (X_8)(X_9)	1500 (X_9)	10.00 (X_8)(X_9)	0.32 (X_4+X_5)	0.32 (X_4+X_5)	20.00 (X_8)(X_9)	X_4 = SF of Ceiling; 1 SF Unit; X_5 = SF of Wall; 1 SF Unit; X_8 = Feet of Track; 1 Track Unit; X_9 = Number of Tracks; 1 Track Unit
8. Lighting						0.04 (X_1)	0.12 (X_1)	0.20 (X_1)	0.20 (X_1)	0.20 (X_1)	X_1 = SF of Floor; 1 SF Unit
9. Police coverage						2,969 (X_1)	5,938 (X_1)	11,875 (X_1)	23,750 (X_1)	47,500 (X_1)	X_1 = SF of Floor; 20,000 SF unit
10. Air conditioning				0.038 (X_3)	0.038 (X_3)	0.038 (X_3)	0.038 (X_3)	0.038 (X_3)	0.038 (X_3)	0.038 (X_3)	X_3 = CF of Station Volume; 1 CF unit
11. Washrooms					156 (X_1)	156 (X_1)	1,798 (X_1)	2,421 (X_1)	6,017 (X_1)	10,858 (X_1)	X_1 = SF of Floor; 20,000 SF unit

*SF = Square Feet
**CF = Cubic Feet

Table 7-2
Measured Values of Selected Environmental Variables

Station	Boro	Location	Lighting	Noise db	Light fc	Station COH	Outside COH	Diff from out. COH
1) Fulton St	Man	Und.	Fluor.	103	3.6	1.27	–	–
2) 50th St-8th Ave	Man	Und.	Fluor.	106	6.1	2.98	–	–
3) 77th St-Lex.	Man	Und.	Fluor.	104	4.4	1.45	–	–
4) Times Sq-42nd St	Man	Und.	Inc.	99	6.1	1.63	2.10	(–) .47
5) 207th St-Bdway	Man	Und.	Fluor.	94	9.4	2.50	1.90	(–) .60
6) 96th St-Lex. Ave.	Man	Und.	Fluor.	108	2.5	2.21	4.30	(–)2.09
7) 7th Ave-53rd St.	Man	Und.	Fluor.	107	7.1	2.18	2.40	(–)0.22
8) 5th Ave.-53rd St.	Man	Und.	Fluor.	106	1.9	1.82	2.40	(–) .58
9) Clinton-Washington	Bklyn	Und.	Inc.	103	1.8	–	0.5	–
10) Myrtle-Bdway	Bklyn	Elev.	Inc.	103	200	–	–	–
11) Norwood Ave.	Bklyn	Elev.	Inc.	–	200	–	–	–
12) 77th-4th Ave.	Bklyn	Und.	Fluor.	104	4.4	2.76	–	–
13) Gates Ave.	Bklyn	Elev.	Inc.	99	200	–	–	–
14) Court St.-Boro/Hall	Bklyn	Und.	Fluor.	102	5.4	.76	0.0	(+) .76
15) E. Pkwy-Bdway Jct.	Bklyn	Elev.	Inc.	99	200	–	–	–
16) Prospect Park	Bklyn	Open	Fluor.	96	200	.29	–	–
17) 45th St-4th Ave.	Bklyn	Und.	Fluor.	111	4.4	.54	1.2	(–) .66
18) Church Ave.	Bklyn	Und.	Fluor.	–	–	1.2	1.4	(–) .20
19) 13th Ave.	Bklyn	Elev.	Inc.	–	200	–	–	–
20) 225th-WPR	Bronx	Elev.	Inc.	–	200	–	–	–
21) 204th-3rd Ave.	Bronx	Elev.	Inc.	–	200	–	–	–
22) Elderts Lane	Queens	Elev.	Inc.	–	200	–	–	–
23) Forest Ave.	Queens	Elev.	Inc.	–	200	–	–	–
24) 71st-Continental	Queens	Und.	Inc.	–	–	–	–	–
25) 80th St-Hudson	Queens	Elev.	Inc.	–	200	–	–	–

Man   = Manhattan   Und. = Underground
Bklyn = Brooklyn   Elev. = Elevated
                         Open = Open Cut

Light was measured with a Miranda-Cadius II light meter, in e.v. units which can be converted to foot candles, at the same position and angle relative to lighting fixtures at each station.

Noise was measured with a General Radio 1551-C Sound Level Meter in "C"

Temperature			Rel. Humidity			Levels	Escalators	Headways		
Sta. °F	Out. °F	Diff from out. °F	Sta. %	Out. %	Diff from out. %			Depth (feet)	Peak Hr (minutes)	Off-Peak
59	40	+19	57	68	−11	3	No	50	1½	30
60	49	+11	73	54	+19	1	No	30	2½	30
49	36.	+13	54	46	+ 8	1	No	20	3	30
50	28	+22	43	32	+11	3	No	50	1½	30
56	34	+22	55	62	−7	1	No	20	2	30
50	37	+13	55	48	+ 7	1	No	20	3	30
64	48	+16	70	60	+10	2	Yes	40	2½	30
63	52	+11	60	57	+ 3	2	Yes	60	1	30
51	50	+1	75	38	+37	1	No	20	2	30
42	42	0	69	69	0	1	No	25	3	30
−	−	−	−	−	−	1	No	25	4	30
47	44	+3	79	49	+30	1	No	20	4	30
44	44	0	56	56	0	1	No	25	4	30
55	−	−	49	−	−	2	Yes	50	2½	30
50	50	0	43	43	0	4	Yes	60	2	30
37	37	0	57	57	0	1	No	15	2½	30
52	40	+12	63	68	−5	1	No	20	4	30
−	−	−	−	−	−	1	No	20	4	30
−	−	−	−	−	−	1	No	25	15	60
−	−	−	−	−	−	1	No	25	2½	30
−	−	−	−	−	−	1	No	25	5	30
−	−	−	−	−	−	1	No	25	4	30
−	−	−	−	−	−	1	No	25	4	30
−	−	−	−	−	−	1	No	30	1	30
−	−	−	−	−	−	1	No	25	2½	30

Fluor. = Fluorescent	db	= decibels
Inc. = Incandescent	fc	= foot-candles
	COH	= Coefficient of Haze

scale overall db readings, also for the same location and conditions in each station, for arriving and for departing trains.

Dirt in the station air was sampled with a Gelman 23000 Paper Tape Air Sampler whose tapes were analyzed on a Gelman 14101 Optical Density Meter in Coefficient of Haze (COH) units.

Temperature and *Relative humidity* were measured both in the station and immediately outside the station (for underground stations) with Nurenberg wet and dry bulb thermometers.

As part of the analysis of the returned survey card data, an analysis of the ambient level measurement was made, with a correlation between responses from various stations and ambient levels from those stations. In addition, air pollution samples from the street level above the stations were obtained from the New York City Air Pollution Bureau of the Environmental Protection Administration (in COH units), and compared to the levels in the stations below. Temperature and humidity levels were compared from station to street level as well as from station to station. The information gathered is summarized in Table 7-2.

Comparisons with Actual Amenity Factor
Measurements Made at Survey Stations
(see Table 7-2)

Convenience

Escalators: Most of the surveyed stations had no escalators, including two which descend three levels.

Train Service: Twenty-one of the twenty-five stations were below the "comfort" level of service of 1 1/2 minutes during the peak hours; none of them reached the 20-minute headway requirement for off-peak service.

Washrooms: Condition of washrooms was not surveyed for this study.

Cleanliness: COH = Coefficient of Haze. The New York City Department of Air Resources considers a rating of 1.0 "unsatisfactory." On this basis, nine of the thirteen stations where air was measured were at least "unsatisfactory," if not "dangerous."

Temperature

No station surveyed was at or near "comfort" level of 72 degrees, but it is apparent that underground stations are warmer than outside temperatures; a boon in winter but a major problem in summer. This is *not*, however, true of all stations in the system.

Noise

All measured stations had noise-level readings greater than "comfort" level, some as high as 106, 107, and 108 db.

Illumination

All underground stations were well below "comfort" level.

Part III
Applying the Method and Evaluating Results

8 Application of the Methodologies

In applying the developed methodologies it was necessary to specify, for the three stations used in the example, the following variables:

Dimensions, as related to environmental amenities; and
Amenity levels existing.

For purposes of this application, Table 8-1 shows the values used.

Also required is the information shown in Table 8-2: dimensions and weighting of environmental amenities. This table includes "overload" (see

Table 8-1
Values Used in Example Calculations

	Station		
Existing Values	1	2	3
Amenity			
1: Cleaning	no cleaning	1 shift/day	1/2 shift/day
2: Escalators	100 ft.	125 ft.	0 ft.
3: Winter temperature	62° F	37° F	62° F
4: Redecoration	need wall, ceiling	Paint 5-year	Furniture
5: Peak hour train service	6-min. headways	1-1/2 min.	4-min.
6: Off-peak train service	30-min. headways	15-min.	10-min.
7: Noise	102 db	88 db	94 db
8: Lighting	<1 f-c	15 f-c	10 f-c
9: Police	16 man-hrs/day	2 man-hrs/day	2 man-hrs/day
10: Summer temperature	97° F	87° F	97° F
11: Washrooms	12 man-hrs/day	6 man-hrs/day	no service
Floor area (square feet)	15,000	20,000	30,000
Ceiling area (square feet)	15,000	22,000	30,000
Wall area (square feet)	16,000	20,000	26,000
Volume (cubic feet)	750,000	900,000	1,300,000
Linear feet of track	450	600	800
Number of tracks	2	4	10
Miles run of train route	15	15	15
Peak hour patron volume	5,682	17,786	36,317

Table 8-2
Dimensions and Weighting of Environmental Amenities

Amenity	Measure	Basic Increment	Overload* Values	Relative Weighting (Among Stations)	Minimum Level of Service
1. Cleaning	Square feet of floor	20,000	10%	ADT	some cleaning
2. Escalators	Peak hour patron volume	6,000	40%	ADT	
3. Heating	Cubic feet of volume	1		ADT	
4. Redecoration					
• Floors	Square feet of floor	1		ADT	
• Ceilings	Square feet of ceiling	1		ADT	
• Walls	Square feet of wall	1		ADT	
• Furnishings	Square feet of floor	20,000		ADT	some furniture
• Painting	Square feet of ceiling	1		ADT	
5. Peak hour train service	Miles of route	1	50%	ΣADT (for all	
6. Off-peak train service	Miles of route	1	50%	ΣADT stations)	
7. Noise					
• Rail lubricators	Number of tracks	1		ADT	
• Resilient rail fasteners	Feet of track; number of tracks	1;1		ADT	
• Floating slab	Feet of track; number of tracks	1;1		ADT	
• Rail grinding	Feet of track; number of tracks	1;1		ADT	
• Acoustic treatment	Square feet of walls & ceilings			ADT	
8. Lighting	Square feet of floor	1		ADT	
9. Police	Square feet of floor	20,000	60%	ADT	some police
10. Air conditioning	Cubic feet of volume	1		ADT	
11. Washrooms	Square feet of volume	20,000	60%	ADT	some service

*Values at which next basic increment invoked, e.g., at 8,400 persons/peak hour *two* escalators justified. These values are deemed appropriate even if first overload not satisfied: every station should have escalator service.

Chapter 7) values to be used in considering such amenities as *escalators:* if peak hour is measured at 8400 patrons, two escalators are required.

All of the foregoing instruction details are of course necessary to the computer program, shown in the Appendix.

Table 8-3 summarizes additional variables required in testing the procedures for three stations: *amenity ratings* (as developed in Chapter 5), the *initial levels* of measured environmental amenities (such as those shown in Table 8-1), and *station weightings*. The station weights are necessary in judging between and among stations, and average annual daily traffic (turnstile counts) is used. It should be noted that the train service amenity entries (numbers 5 and 6) will be assigned to one station (Station 1) for ease of computation; in actuality the cost of improvement of a *route* amenity (train service) would be apportioned among the stations it serves.

Having entered all relevant values and computational instructions, Table 8-4 is the first produced. This table lists actual costs for each amenity at each station (Station 1 = Amenity 1 through 11; Station 2 = 12 through 22; Station 3 = 23 through 33; Amenity 1 = Amenity 12 = Amenity 23). This cost is *not* the decision variable (this was previously discussed).

From this point, *methodology 1* produces the calculations shown in Tables 8-5A, B, and C, for multiples of R^{**}, and *methodology 2* produces the single Table 8-6.

It may be noted that while these methodologies are both to be applied in the expenditure of a predetermined amount of money, each of the calculations was brought to completion, i.e., to the point of taking each and every amenity to *comfort*, or *Level 1*. By this means, the mechanics of incremental expenditure may be examined more closely, as will be done in Chapter 9.

Table 8-3
Summary of Ratings, Levels, Weightings

Station	Amenity	Rating	Initial Level*	Station Weight
	1	.17	6	
	2	.15	5	
	3	.13	3	
	4	.12	2	
1	5	.11	4	21,400**
	6	.11	4	
	7	.08	6	
	8	.08	2	
	9	.07	6	
	10	.06	7	
	11	.03	1	
	1(12)	.17	3	
	2(13)	.15	6	
	3(14)	.13	8	
	4(15)	.12	5	
	5(16)	.11	1	
2	6(17)	.11	2	32,354
	7(18)	.08	2	
	8(19)	.08	1	
	9(20)	.07	5	
	10(21)	.06	4	
	11(22)	.03	2	
	1(23)	.17	4	
	2(24)	.15	1	
	3(25)	.13	7	
	4(26)	.12	4	
	5(27)	.11	3	
3	6(28)	.11	1	43,583
	7(29)	.08	4	
	8(30)	.08	2	
	9(31)	.07	5	
	10(32)	.06	6	
	11(33)	.03	7	

*Based on information specified as part of the case in Table 6-1.
**Annual Average Daily Traffic; in some cases only weekday (or only weekend) values might be more appropriate.

Table 8-4
Costs (D_{ij}) Per Amenity Level

LISTING OF COSTS...AMENITIES VERTICAL...LEVELS HORIZONTAL

	11	10	9	8	7	6	5	4	3	2	1
1	0.	0.	0.	0.	0.	938.	1875.	3750.	7500.	15000.	
2	0.	0.	0.	10000.	10000.	10000.	10000.	10000.	10000.	10000.	
3	0.	30000.	30000.	30000.	30000.	30000.	30000.	30000.	30000.	30000.	
4	0.	0.	0.	150.	75.	225.	350.	1950.	1760.	3750.	
5	0.	0.	0.	0.	0.	0.	184995.	300000.	549990.	979995.	
6	0.	0.	0.	0.	0.	0.	274995.	274995.	274995.	549990.	
7	0.	0.	0.	0.	0.	72.	3000.	9000.	9920.	18000.	
8	0.	0.	0.	0.	0.	0.	600.	1800.	3000.	3000.	
9	0.	0.	0.	0.	0.	2969.	5938.	11875.	23750.	47500.	
10	0.	0.	0.	0.	28500.	28500.	28500.	28500.	28500.	28500.	
11	0.	0.	0.	0.	156.	156.	1798.	2421.	6017.	10858.	
12	0.	0.	0.	0.	0.	938.	1875.	3750.	7500.	15000.	
13	0.	0.	0.	30000.	30000.	30000.	30000.	30000.	30000.	30000.	
14	0.	36000.	36000.	36000.	36000.	36000.	36000.	36000.	36000.	36000.	
15	0.	0.	0.	220.	110.	330.	700.	2600.	2200.	5500.	
16	0.	0.	0.	0.	0.	0.	184995.	300000.	549990.	979995.	
17	0.	0.	0.	0.	0.	0.	274995.	274995.	274995.	549990.	
18	0.	0.	0.	0.	0.	192.	6000.	24000.	13440.	48000.	
19	0.	0.	0.	0.	0.	0.	800.	2400.	4000.	4000.	
20	0.	0.	0.	0.	0.	2969.	5938.	11875.	23750.	47500.	
21	0.	0.	0.	0.	34200.	34200.	34200.	34200.	34200.	34200.	
22	0.	0.	0.	0.	156.	156.	1798.	2421.	6017.	10858.	
23	0.	0.	0.	0.	0.	1876.	3750.	7500.	15000.	30000.	
24	0.	0.	0.	60000.	60000.	60000.	60000.	60000.	60000.	60000.	
25	0.	52000.	52000.	52000.	52000.	52000.	52000.	52000.	52000.	52000.	
26	0.	0.	0.	300.	150.	450.	700.	3900.	2860.	7500.	
27	0.	0.	0.	0.	0.	0.	184995.	300000.	549990.	979995.	
28	0.	0.	0.	0.	0.	0.	274995.	274995.	274995.	549990.	
29	0.	0.	0.	0.	0.	640.	15000.	80000.	17920.	160000.	
30	0.	0.	0.	0.	0.	0.	1200.	3600.	6000.	6000.	
31	0.	0.	0.	0.	0.	2969.	5938.	11875.	23750.	47500.	
32	0.	0.	0.	0.	49400.	49400.	49400.	49400.	49400.	49400.	
33	0.	0.	0.	0.	156.	156.	1798.	2421.	6017.	10858.	

Note: These are not design variables but indicate actual costs for example stations.

Table 8-5A
Method 1: Expenditures at Indicated Multiples of R** (1 through 8)

	1		2		3		4	
AMENITY	LEVELS MOVED	COST	LEVELS MOVED	COST	LEVELS MOVED	COST	LEVELS MOVED	COST
1	5	29063.	5	29063.	5	29063.	5	29063.
2	2	20000.	4	40000.	4	40000.	4	40000.
3	0	0.	1	30000.	1	30000.	1	30000.
4	1	3750.	1	3750.	1	3750.	1	3750.
5	0	0.	0	0.	0	0.	0	0.
6	0	0.	0	0.	0	0.	0	0.
7	2	3072.	3	12072.	5	39992.	5	39992.
8	1	3000.	1	3000.	1	3000.	1	3000.
9	1	2969.	1	2969.	2	8907.	2	8907.
10	0	0.	1	28500.	1	28500.	2	57000.
11	0	0.	0	0.	0	0.	0	0.
12	1	7500.	2	22500.	2	22500.	2	22500.
13	1	30000.	2	60000.	2	60000.	3	90000.
14	1	36000.	2	72000.	2	72000.	3	108000.
15	4	11000.	4	11000.	4	11000.	4	11000.
16	0	0.	0	0.	0	0.	0	0.
17	0	0.	0	0.	0	0.	0	0.
18	0	0.	0	0.	0	0.	0	0.
19	0	0.	0	0.	0	0.	0	0.
20	0	0.	1	5938.	1	5938.	2	17813.
21	0	0.	0	0.	0	0.	1	34200.
22	0	0.	0	0.	0	0.	0	0.
23	1	7500.	2	22500.	3	52500.	3	52500.
24	0	0.	0	0.	0	0.	0	0.
25	0	0.	1	52000.	1	52000.	2	104000.
26	2	6760.	3	14260.	3	14260.	3	14260.
27	0	0.	0	0.	0	0.	0	0.
28	0	0.	0	0.	0	0.	0	0.
29	0	0.	0	0.	0	0.	0	0.
30	0	0.	1	6000.	1	6000.	1	6000.
31	0	0.	1	5938.	1	5938.	2	17813.
32	0	0.	0	0.	1	49400.	1	49400.
33	2	312.	3	2110.	5	10548.	6	21406.
	************		************		************		************	
	SUM =	160927.	SUM =	423601.	SUM =	545297.	SUM =	760605.

	5		6		7		8	
AMENITY	LEVELS MOVED	COST	LEVELS MOVED	COST	LEVELS MOVED	COST	LEVELS MOVED	COST
1	5	29063.	5	29063.	5	29063.	5	29063.
2	4	40000.	4	40000.	4	40000.	4	40000.
3	1	30000.	2	60000.	2	60000.	2	60000.
4	1	3750.	1	3750.	1	3750.	1	3750.
5	0	0.	0	0.	0	0.	0	0.
6	0	0.	0	0.	0	0.	0	0.
7	5	39992.	5	39992.	5	39992.	5	39992.
8	1	3000.	1	3000.	1	3000.	1	3000.
9	3	20782.	4	44532.	4	44532.	5	92032.
10	2	57000.	2	57000.	3	85500.	3	85500.
11	0	0.	0	0.	0	0.	0	0.
12	2	22500.	2	22500.	2	22500.	2	22500.
13	4	120000.	5	150000.	5	150000.	5	150000.
14	4	144000.	5	180000.	5	180000.	6	216000.
15	4	11000.	4	11000.	4	11000.	4	11000.
16	0	0.	0	0.	0	0.	0	0.
17	0	0.	0	0.	0	0.	0	0.
18	0	0.	0	0.	0	0.	0	0.
19	0	0.	0	0.	0	0.	0	0.
20	2	17813.	2	17813.	3	41563.	3	41563.
21	1	34200.	1	34200.	1	34200.	1	34200.
22	0	0.	1	10858.	1	10858.	1	10858.
23	3	52500.	3	52500.	3	52500.	3	52500.
24	0	0.	0	0.	0	0.	0	0.
25	2	104000.	3	156000.	3	156000.	4	208000.
26	3	14260.	3	14260.	3	14260.	3	14260.
27	0	0.	0	0.	0	0.	0	0.
28	0	0.	0	0.	0	0.	0	0.
29	0	0.	1	80000.	1	80000.	1	80000.
30	1	6000.	1	6000.	1	6000.	1	6000.
31	2	17813.	2	17813.	3	41563.	3	41563.
32	1	49400.	1	49400.	1	49400.	2	98800.
33	6	21406.	6	21406.	6	21406.	6	21406.
	************		************		************		************	
	SUM =	838480.	SUM =	1101087.	SUM =	1177086.	SUM =	1361985.

Table 8-5B
Method 1: Expenditures at Indicated multiples of R** (9, 10, 12, 14, 15, 16, 18, 19)

	9		10		12		14	
AMENITY	LEVELS MOVED	COST	LEVELS MOVED	COST	LEVELS MOVED	COST	LEVELS MOVED	COST
1	5	29063.	5	29063.	5	29063.	5	29063.
2	4	40000.	4	40000.	4	40000.	4	40000.
3	2	60000.	2	60000.	2	60000.	2	69000.
4	1	3750.	1	3750.	1	3750.	1	3750.
5	0	0.	0	0.	0	0.	0	0.
6	0	0.	0	0.	0	0.	0	0.
7	5	39992.	5	39992.	5	39992.	5	39992.
8	1	3000.	1	3000.	1	3000.	1	3000.
9	5	92032.	5	92032.	5	92032.	5	92032.
10	4	114000.	4	114000.	5	142500.	5	142500.
11	0	0.	0	0.	0	0.	0	0.
12	2	22500.	2	22500.	2	22500.	2	22500.
13	5	150000.	5	150000.	5	150000.	5	150000.
14	7	252000.	7	252000.	7	252000.	7	252000.
15	4	11000.	4	11000.	4	11000.	4	11000.
16	0	0.	0	0.	0	0.	0	0.
17	0	0.	0	0.	0	0.	0	0.
18	0	0.	1	48000.	1	48000.	1	48000.
19	0	0.	0	0.	0	0.	0	0.
20	4	89063.	4	89063.	4	89063.	4	89063.
21	1	34200.	2	68400.	2	68400.	2	68400.
22	1	10858.	1	10858.	1	10858.	1	10858.
23	3	52500.	3	52500.	3	52500.	3	52500.
24	0	0.	0	0.	0	0.	0	0.
25	4	208000.	5	260000.	6	312000.	6	312000.
26	3	14260.	3	14260.	3	14260.	3	14260.
27	0	0.	0	0.	0	0.	0	0.
28	0	0.	0	0.	0	0.	0	0.
29	1	80000.	1	80000.	1	80000.	1	80000.
30	1	6000.	1	6000.	1	6000.	1	6000.
31	4	89063.	4	89063.	4	89063.	4	89063.
32	2	98800.	2	98800.	2	98800.	3	148200.
33	6	21406.	6	21406.	6	21406.	6	21406.
	************		************		************		************	
	SUM = 1521485.		SUM = 1655685.		SUM = 1736185.		SUM = 1785585.	

	15		16		19		18	
AMENITY	LEVELS MOVED	COST	LEVELS MOVED	COST	LEVELS MOVED	COST	LEVELS MOVED	COST
1	5	29063.	5	29063.	5	29063.	5	29063.
2	4	40000.	4	40000.	4	40000.	4	40000.
3	2	60000.	2	60000.	2	60000.	2	60000.
4	1	3750.	1	3750.	1	3750.	1	3750.
5	0	0.	0	0.	0	0.	0	0.
6	0	0.	0	0.	1	274995.	1	274995.
7	5	39992.	5	39992.	5	39992.	5	39992.
8	1	3000.	1	3000.	1	3000.	1	3000.
9	5	92032.	5	92032.	5	92032.	5	92032.
10	6	171000.	6	171000.	6	171000.	6	171000.
11	0	0.	0	0.	0	0.	0	0.
12	2	22500.	2	22500.	2	22500.	2	22500.
13	5	150000.	5	150000.	5	150000.	5	150000.
14	7	252000.	7	252000.	7	252000.	7	252000.
15	4	11000.	4	11000.	4	11000.	4	11000.
16	0	0.	0	0.	0	0.	0	0.
17	0	0.	0	0.	0	0.	0	0.
18	1	48000.	1	48000.	1	48000.	1	48000.
19	0	0.	0	0.	0	0.	0	0.
20	4	89063.	4	89063.	4	89063.	4	89063.
21	2	68400.	3	102600.	3	102600.	3	102600.
22	1	10858.	1	10858.	1	10858.	1	10858.
23	3	52500.	3	52500.	3	52500.	3	52500.
24	0	0.	0	0.	0	0.	0	0.
25	6	312000.	6	312000.	6	312000.	6	312000.
26	3	14260.	3	14260.	3	14260.	3	14260.
27	0	0.	0	0.	0	0.	0	0.
28	0	0.	0	0.	0	0.	0	0.
29	1	80000.	1	80000.	2	97920.	2	97920.
30	1	6000.	1	6000.	1	6000.	1	6000.
31	4	89063.	4	89063.	4	89063.	4	89063.
32	3	148200.	3	148200.	4	197600.	3	148200.
33	6	21406.	6	21406.	6	21406.	6	21406.
	************		************		************		************	
	SUM = 1814085.		SUM = 1848285.		SUM = 2190598.		SUM = 2141198.	

Table 8-5C

Method 1: Expenditures at Indicated Multiples of R (24, 30, 54, 90, 150)**

AMENITY	24		30		54		90		150	
	LEVELS MOVED	COST	LEVELS MOVED	COST	LEVELS MOVED	COST	LEVELS MOVED	COST	LEVELS MOVED	COST
1	5	29063.	5	29063.	5	29063.	5	29063.	5	29063.
2	4	40000.	4	40000.	4	40000.	4	40000.	4	40000.
3	2	60000.	2	60000.	2	60000.	2	60000.	2	60000.
4	1	3750.	1	3750.	1	3750.	1	3750.	1	3750.
5	0		1	300000.	2	300000.	2	849990.	3	1829985.
6	1	274995.	1	274995.	2	549990.	3	1099980.	3	1099980.
7	5	39992.	5	39992.	5	39992.	5	39992.	5	39992.
8	1	3000.	1	3000.	1	3000.	1	3000.	1	3000.
9	5	92032.	5	92032.	5	92032.	5	92032.	5	92032.
10	6	171000.	6	171000.	6	171000.	6	171000.	6	171000.
11	0	0.	0	0.	0	0.	0	0.	0	0.
12	2	22500.	2	22500.	2	22500.	2	22500.	2	22500.
13	5	150000.	5	150000.	5	150000.	5	150000.	5	150000.
14	7	252000.	7	252000.	7	252000.	7	252000.	7	252000.
15	4	11000.	4	11000.	4	11000.	4	11000.	4	11000.
16	0	0.	0	0.	0	0.	0	0.	0	0.
17	0	0.	0	0.	1	48000.	0	0.	0	0.
18	1	48000.	1	48000.	0	0.	1	48000.	1	48000.
19	0	0.	0	0.	0	0.	0	0.	3	0.
20	4	89063.	4	89063.	4	89063.	4	89063.	4	89063.
21	3	102600.	3	102600.	3	102600.	3	102600.	3	102600.
22	3	10858.	3	10858.	3	10858.	1	10858.	1	10858.
23	3	52500.	3	52500.	3	52500.	3	52500.	3	52500.
24	0	0.	0	0.	0	0.	0	0.	0	0.
25	6	312000.	6	312000.	6	312000.	6	312000.	6	312000.
26	3	14260.	3	14260.	3	14260.	3	14260.	3	14260.
27	0	0.	0	0.	0	0.	0	0.	0	0.
28	0	0.	0	0.	0	0.	0	0.	0	0.
29	2	97920.	3	257920.	3	257920.	3	257920.	3	257920.
30	1	6000.	1	6000.	1	6000.	1	6000.	1	6000.
31	4	89063.	4	89063.	4	89063.	4	89063.	4	89063.
32	5	247000.	5	247000.	5	247000.	5	247000.	5	247000.
33	6	21406.	6	21406.	6	21406.	6	21406.	6	21406.
	************		*************		************		*************		************	
	SUM = 22399998.		SUM = 2699997.		SUM = 2974992.		SUM = 4074970.		SUM = 5054965.	

Table 8-6
Method 2: Expenditures by Transition From Selected Amenity Levels

TRANSITION RECORD	AMENITY FROM LEVEL	TO LEVEL	WEIGHT	COST	CUMULATIVE COST
7	6	5	0.12E 03	72.	72.
33	7	6	0.50E 02	156.	228.
33	6	5	0.42E 02	156.	384.
15	5	4	0.22E 02	700.	1084.
1	6	5	0.19E 02	938.	2022.
1	5	4	0.78E 01	1875.	3897.
15	4	3	0.45E 01	2600.	6497.
26	4	3	0.40E 01	3900.	10397.
26	3	2	0.37E 01	2860.	13257.
15	3	2	0.35E 01	2200.	15457.
23	4	3	0.30E 01	7500.	22957.
1	4	3	0.29E 01	3750.	26707.
33	5	4	0.29E 01	1798.	28505.
9	6	5	0.25E 01	2969.	31474.
7	5	4	0.23E 01	3000.	34474.
31	5	4	0.21E 01	5938.	40412.
33	4	3	0.16E 01	2421.	42833.
20	5	4	0.15E 01	5938.	48771.
12	3	2	0.15E 01	7500.	56271.
2	5	4	0.13E 01	10000.	66271.
9	5	4	0.10E 01	5938.	72209.
23	3	2	0.99E 00	15000.	87209.
1	3	2	0.97E 00	7500.	94709.
2	4	3	0.96E 00	10000.	104709.
14	8	7	0.82E 00	36000.	140709.
13	6	5	0.81E 00	30000.	170709.
31	4	3	0.77E 00	11875.	182584.
15	2	1	0.71E 00	5500.	188085.
14	7	6	0.70E 00	36000.	224085.
26	2	1	0.70E 00	7500.	231585.
4	2	1	0.68E 00	3750.	235335.
25	7	6	0.65E 00	52000.	287335.
13	5	4	0.65E 00	30000.	317335.
2	3	2	0.64E 00	10000.	327335.
14	6	5	0.58E 00	36000.	363335.
30	2	1	0.58E 00	6000.	369335.
20	4	3	0.57E 00	11875.	381210.
8	2	1	0.57E 00	3000.	384210.
7	4	3	0.57E 00	9000.	393210.
25	6	5	0.54E 00	52000.	445210.
13	4	3	0.49E 00	30000.	475210.
14	5	4	0.47E 00	36000.	511210.
25	5	4	0.44E 00	52000.	563210.
33	3	2	0.43E 00	6017.	569227.
9	4	3	0.38E 00	11875.	581102.
12	2	1	0.37E 00	15000.	596102.
14	4	3	0.35E 00	36000.	632102.
7	3	2	0.35E 00	9920.	642022.
25	4	3	0.33E 00	52000.	694022.
13	3	2	0.32E 00	30000.	724022.
2	2	1	0.32E 00	10000.	734022.
10	7	6	0.27E 00	28500.	762522.
32	6	5	0.26E 00	49400.	811922.
31	3	2	0.26E 00	23750.	835672.
23	2	1	0.25E 00	30000.	865672.
1	2	1	0.24E 00	15000.	880672.
14	3	2	0.23E 00	36000.	916672.
10	6	5	0.23E 00	28500.	945172.
25	3	2	0.22E 00	52000.	997172.
32	5	4	0.21E 00	49400.	1046572.
20	3	2	0.19E 00	23750.	1070321.
3	3	2	0.19E 00	30000.	1100321.
10	5	4	0.18E 00	28500.	1128820.
21	4	3	0.17E 00	34200.	1163019.
13	2	1	0.16E 00	30000.	1193019.
32	4	3	0.16E 00	49400.	1242418.
10	4	3	0.14E 00	28500.	1270917.
29	4	3	0.13E 00	80000.	1350917.
29	3	2	0.13E 00	17920.	1368836.
9	3	2	0.13E 00	23750.	1392586.
33	2	1	0.12E 00	10858.	1403444.
14	2	1	0.12E 00	36000.	1439444.
6	4	3	0.12E 00	274995.	1714439.
21	3	2	0.11E 00	34200.	1748638.
25	2	1	0.11E 00	52000.	1800638.
5	4	3	0.11E 00	300000.	2100638.
32	3	2	0.11E 00	49400.	2150037.
7	2	1	0.95E-01	18000.	2168037.
3	2	1	0.93E-01	30000.	2198037.
10	3	2	0.90E-01	28500.	2226536.
22	2	1	0.89E-01	10858.	2237394.
6	3	2	0.78E-01	274995.	2512389.
31	2	1	0.64E-01	47500.	2559889.
21	2	1	0.57E-01	34200.	2594088.
18	2	1	0.54E-01	48000.	2642088.
32	2	1	0.53E-01	49400.	2691487.
20	2	1	0.48E-01	47500.	2738987.
10	2	1	0.45E-01	28500.	2767486.
5	3	2	0.39E-01	549990.	3317476.
9	2	1	0.32E-01	47500.	3364976.
29	2	1	0.22E-01	160000.	3524976.
6	2	1	0.19E-01	549990.	4074966.
5	2	1	0.11E-01	979995.	5054961.

9

A Review of the Results

Analysis

From Tables 8-5A, B, and C, for methodology 1, and from Table 8-6, for methodology 2, a series of figures was constructed for the purpose of determining the relative merits of the two methods.

Figure 9-1 gives the spending pattern of Method 1, rising quickly to about $2,000,000, then meeting resistance at successive multiples of the normalized R^{**} used in that methodology. Resistance "plateaus" are met at 10, 12, 16, 19, 24, 30, 54, 90 and $150R^{**}$. These points will be discussed further.

Figure 9-2 shows the more gradual spending pattern of Method 2, in which $2,000,000 is reached at about the 3/4 point in total spending, rather than about the 1/4 point as in Method 1. Table 9-1 compares the number of levels moved by the two methodologies in their first 33 choices. Method 1 is constrained by its formulation to consider all amenities at the same time (by successive multiples of R^{**}), while Method 2 seeks individual values. In comparing the first iteration of R^{**} to the first 33 choices of Method 2, it is seen that for Station 1 there is no advantage (in levels moved) for each method; for Station 2, Method 2 has moved two levels beyond Method 1; and for Station 3, Method 2 has moved seven levels beyond. However, at this point Method 1 has expended $160,927, and Method 2 has spent $317,335.

Another comparison is made of history of amenity improvement, level by level, over the entire expenditure range. Figure 9-3, for Station 1, shows that the improvement of each amenity is quite close in pattern for both methodologies, but that generally the last improvements (to comfort) are delayed by Method 2. Figure 9-4 shows a similar pattern for Station 2, with early levels satisfied *earlier* in many cases by Method 2, but the last few levels delayed. Figure 9-5 is a similar record for Station 3.

Table 9-2 presents a comparison of amenity levels moved in each methodology, at each "plateau" seen in Figure 9-1. These plateaus show a certain resistance against expenditure by Method 1, providing bench-marks of diminishing returns. Table 9-2 shows, at Plateau 1, Method 1 overwhelmingly ahead of Method 2 (by eight amenity levels) at this earliest point of expenditure resistance. At Plateau 2, Method 1 is slightly ahead; at Plateaus 3 and 4 (about $2,000,000) there is no apparent difference in movement. In succeeding plateaus, Method 2 moves ahead in numbers of levels moved. All of this again

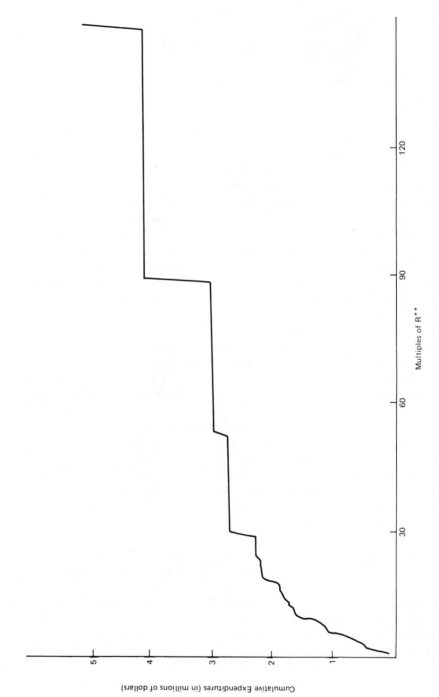

Figure 9-1. Methodology 1: Expenditures by Multiples of Normalized R** (Cumulative)

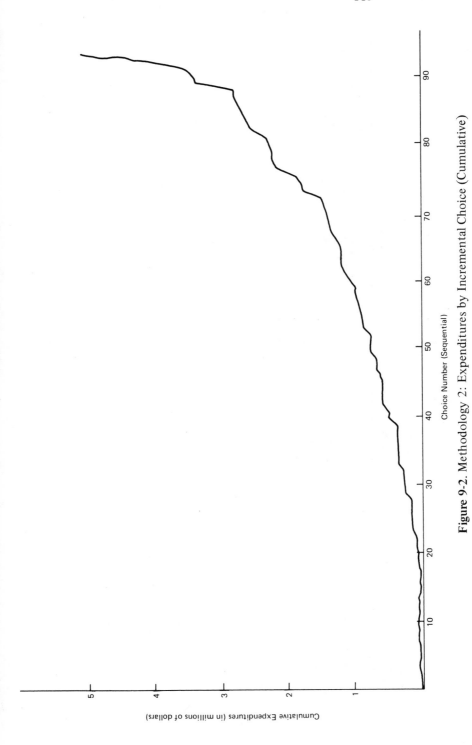

Figure 9-2. Methodology 2: Expenditures by Incremental Choice (Cumulative)

Table 9-1
Comparison of R** of Method 1 with First 33 Choices of Method 2

Amenity	Station 1			Station 2			Station 3		
	Method 1	Method 2	2 minus 1	Method 1	Method 2	2 minus 1	Method 1	Method 2	2 minus 1
1: Cleaning	5	4	−1	1	1	0	1	2	+1
2: Escalators	2	2	0	1	2	+1	0	0	0
3: Heating	0	0	0	1	2	+1	0	1	+1
4: Redecoration	1	1	0	4	3	−1	2	3	+1
5: Peak hour trains	0	0	0	0	0	0	0	0	0
6: Off-peak trains	0	0	0	0	0	0	0	0	0
7: Noise	2	2	0	0	0	0	0	0	0
8: Light	1	0	0	0	0	0	0	0	0
9: Police	1	2	+1	0	1	+1	0	2	+2
10: Cooling	0	0	0	0	0	0	0	0	0
11: Washrooms	0	0	0	0	0	0	2	4	+2
TOTAL			0			+2			+7

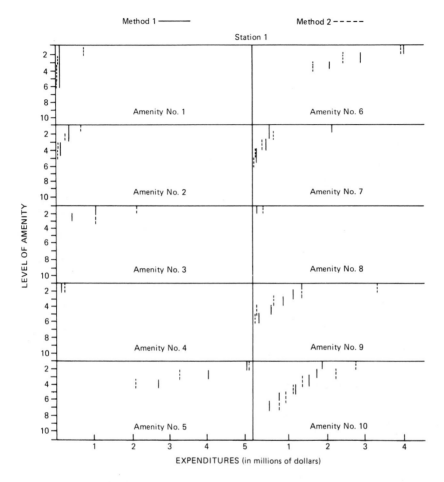

Figure 9-3. Comparison of Expenditures by Amenity, by Level (Station 1)

illustrates the history of expenditure seen in Figures 9-1 and 9-2: Methodology 1 expends its funds somewhat more efficiently (from the standpoint of moving a greater number of levels for the same amount of money) than does Method 2.

Evaluation

Both methodologies utilize the same basic approach, Equation (4.5):

$$\mu_{ij} = \frac{R_i}{d_{ij}} (j - 1)$$

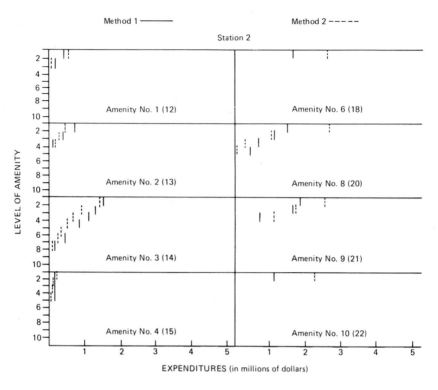

Figure 9-4. Comparison of Expenditures by Amenity, by Level (Station 2)

But Method 1 uses *average* cost in its denominator while Method 2 puts each cost d_{ij} in the denominator to form μ_{ij}; this may explain the differences in behavior. However, the basic difference in *application* is that Method 1 *forces* acceptance of each incremental amenity improvement (unless the R^{**} factor is too small to demand a unit), while Method 2 *chooses* among all weighted, costed increments for the smallest number.

To determine precisely how the differences operate, Table 9-3 is prepared, which lists, in order of decreasing importance, the three elements of the basic formulation: initial level (worst first), patron rating (highest first), and cost (overall cost of needed improvement; cheapest first). By rating the choices made by each methodology, a numerical comparison can be made.

Table 9-4 rates those choices, from Figures 9-3, 9-4 and 9-5, rating (on the basis of Table 9-2) those amenities which are satisfied (taken to comfort) by Method 1 or Method 2. Table 9-4 shows that, on the average, Method 1 has taken to completion those amenities which are:

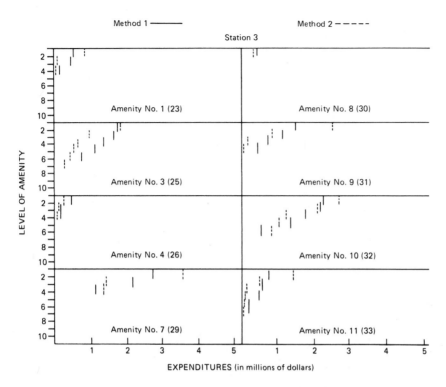

Figure 9-5. Comparison of Expenditures by Amenity, by Level (Station 3)

slightly less distant from comfort
less highly rated by the public
somewhat cheaper

than the amenities completed by Method 2.

However, since Method 1 has taken to comfort first so many more amenities than has Method 2 (21 versus 5), this last comparison may have limited applicability.

The conclusion to be drawn is that Method 1 favors, to some degree, choice by cost, while Method 2 favors, to a lesser degree, choice by level, and by rating. A clear choice of methodology, then, cannot be made except where one element or the other, *level* (or distance from comfort) or *cost* is to be favored.

In sum, Method 1 satisfies more amenities than Method 2, but presents a need for more repetitive computational operations, a minimal point if machine-programmed, and such programming is available for practical application.

Table 9-2
Comparison of Amenity Levels Moved by Methods 1 and 2 at Each Funding Plateau

Amenity	Method 1	Method 2	Plateau 1 (10R**) $1,655,685 2 minus 1	Plateau 2 (12R**) $1,736,185 Method 1	2 minus 1	Plateau 3 (16R**) $1,848,285 2 minus 1	Plateau 4 (19R**) $2,190,598 Method 1	2 minus 1	Plateau 5 (24R**) $2,239,998 Method 1	2 minus 1	Plateau 6 (30R**) $2,699,997 Method 1	2 minus 1	Plateau 7 (54R**) $2,974,992 Method 1	2 minus 1	Plateau 8 (90R**) $4,074,970 Method 1	2 minus 1	Plateau 9 (150R**) $5,054,965 Method 1	2 minus 1
1	5	5	—												1	+1	1	+1
2	4	4													1	0		–1
3	2	1	–1												1	–1	1	
4	1	1					1	+1	1	+1	1	–1						
5	0	0		1	+1		1	–1			1	0	1	–1	1			
6	0	0					1	+1										
7	5	4	–1															
8	1	1												+1	1	+1		
9	5	4	–1															
10	4	4		1	–1	–1			1	+1			1	+1				
11	0	0																
12	2	2																
13	5	5																
14	7	7																
15	4	4																
16	0	0																
17	0	0																
18	1	0									1	+1						

19	0	0									
20	4	2	−2				−1			+1	
21	2	1	−1								
22	1	0	−1			0		+1	+1		−1
23	3	3									
24	0	0									
25	5	4	−1		−1	+1					+1
26	3	3									
27	0	0									
28	0	0									
29	1	2	+1		+1		−1	−1	+1 +1		
30	1	1									
31	4	3	−1		3		0				
32	2	2									
33	6	6									
TOTAL			−8	−1	0	0	+2	+3	+1	+2	0

Table 9-3
Ordering of Elements of Allocation Index

Order	Initial Level[a]	Patron Rating[b]	Cost[c]
1	14[d]	1[d],12,23	8[d]
2	10,25,33	2,13,24	4
3	1,7,9,13,32	3,14,25	30
4	2,15,20,31	4,15,26	22
5	5,6,21,23,26,29	5,6,16,17,27,28	15
6	3,12,27	7,8,18,19,29,30	26
7	4,8,17,18,22,30	9,20,31	33
8	11,16,19,24,28	10,21,32	12
9		11,22,33	1
10			7
11			2
12			18
13			23
14			3
15			20,31
16			9
17			21
18			13
19			10
20			32
21			14
22			29
23			25
24			17
25			6
26			27
27			5

[a]in descending order: 8,7,6,5,4,3,2,1
[b]in descending order: .17,.15,.13,.12,.11,.08,.07,.06,.03
[c]in order of increasing cost: $3,000, 3,750, 6,000, 10,858, 11,000, 14,260, 21,406, 22,50, 29,063, 39,992, 40,000, 48,000, 52,500, 60,000, 89,063, 92,032, 102,600, 150,000, 171,000, 247,000, 252,000, 257,920, 312,000, 549,990, 1,099,980, 1,529,985, 1,829,985
[d]amenity numbers

Table 9-4
Performance Rating of Methodologies

	Method 1 satisfies first			Method 2 satisfies first		
Amenity	Level[a]	Rating[b]	Cost[c]	Level	Rating	Cost
1: Cleaning	3	1	9			
2: Escalators	4	2	11			
3: Heating	6	3	14			
4: Redecoration	7	4	2			
5: Peak hr. trains	5	5	27			
6: Off-peak hr. trns				5	5	25
7: Noise	3	6	10			
8: Light	7	6	1			
9: Police	3	7	16			
10: Cooling	2	8	19			
12: Cleaning	6	1	8			
13: Escalators				3	2	18
14: Heating				1	3	21
15: Redecoration	4	4	5			
18: Noise	7	6	12			
20: Police	4	7	15			
21: Cooling	5	8	17			
22: Washrooms	7	9	4			
23: Cleaning	5	1	13			
25: Heating	2	3	23			
26: Redecoration				5	4	6
29: Noise	5	6	22			
30: Light				7	6	3
31: Police	4	7	15			
32: Cooling	3	8	20			
33: Washrooms	2	9	7			
Σ	94	111	270	21	20	73
$\bar{x}$	4.5	4.5	12.9	4.2	4.0	14.6

[a],[b],[c]ratings from Table 9-3

Appendix

Appendix: Notes on Analytical Method

Since the data could be classified according to three variables, it is exhibited most advantageously in a three-dimensional array, $Y(i, j, k)$, the first subscript referring to the station number (or group of stations category), the second to the rank of the response, and the third to the number of the amenity category.

The variations throughout this array can be expressed in components that can be attributed to the differences in ranks according to the station where the questionnaire was received, $R(i)$, the difference in rank attributed to a specific improvement by those questioned, $C(j)$, the difference in rank at a particular station due to something different about the station, e.g., new lighting, escalators, etc., $T(i, j)$, and other differences not covered in the other effects, $E(i, j, k)$. Expressing the above mathematically results in:

$$Y(i,j,k) = M + R(i) + C(j) + T(i,j) + E(i,j,k) \qquad (A.1)$$

which is a linear model. To develop the variation from the mean M, the sample variance is computed thus:

$$S^2 = \sum_{ijk} (Y_{ijk} - M)^2/(N-1) \qquad (A.2)$$

This sample variance, S^2, is then broken up into sources of variation, as was done with $Y(i,j,k)$. The results have been stated in an analysis of variance table, which follows.

Table Appendix-1
Distribution of Questionnaires and Returns

No.	Station Name	Number Distributed	Number Returned	Percent Returned
1	Fulton Street (Manh.)	1000	173	17.3
2	50th St. - 8th Ave. (Manh.)	1000	141	14.1
3	77th St. - Lexington Ave. (Manh.)	1000	257	25.7
4	Times Sq. - 42nd St. (Manh.)	1000	191	19.1
5	207th - 8th Ave. (Manh.)	776	201	25.9
6	96th St. - Lexington Ave. (Manh.)	1000	168	16.8
7	7th Ave. - 53rd St. (Manh.)	1000	261	26.1
8	5th Ave. - 53rd St. (Manh.)	1000	254	25.4
9	Clinton - Washington (Bklyn.)	908	52	5.7
10	Myrtle - Broadway (Bklyn.)	1000	61	6.1
11	Norwood Ave. (Bklyn.)	426	62	14.6
12	77th St. - 4th Ave. (Bklyn.)	523	191	36.5
13	Gates Ave. - Broadway (Bklyn.)	973	96	9.9
14	Court St. - Boro Hall (Bklyn.)	1000	214	21.4
15	Eastern Parkway - Broadway Jn. (Bklyn.)	1000	80	8.0
16	Prospect Park (Bklyn.)	773	102	13.2
17	45th St. - 4th Ave. (Bklyn.)	515	75	14.6
18	Church Ave. (Bklyn.)	1000	179	17.9
19	13th Ave. - Ditmas Ave. (Bklyn.)	200	12	6.0
20	225th St. - White Plains Road (Bronx)	958	65	6.8
21	204th St. - 3rd Ave. (Bronx)	200	79	39.5
22	Elberts Lane (Queens)	490	140	28.6
23	Forest Ave. (Queens)	662	110	16.6
24	71st St. - Continental Ave. (Queens)	1000	201	20.1
25	80th St. - Hudson St. (Queens)	660	136	20.6
	TOTAL	20,000	3,678	18.4

Table Appendix-2
Analysis of Variance: Methodology

	Sum of Squares	Degrees of Freedom	Mean Square	F-Ratios
Column Means	$S_c = r_i \, \Sigma n_i \, (Y_{i\cdot\cdot} - Y_{\cdots})^2$	$c-1$	$M_c = S_c/(c-1)$	M_c/M_w
Row Means	$S_r = c_i \, \Sigma n_i (Y_{\cdot j\cdot} - Y_{\cdots})^2$	$r-1$	$M_r = S_r/(r-1)$	M_r/M_w
Interaction	$S_i = S_s - s_r - S_c$	$(c-1)(r-1)$	$M_i = S_i/[(c-1)(r-1)]$	M_i/M_w
Subtotal	$S_s = \Sigma \, n_i \, (Y_{ij\cdot} - Y_{\cdots})^2$	$rc-1$	$M_s = S_s/(rc-1)$	
Within	$S_w = S_t - S_s$	$\Sigma n_i - rc$	$M_w = S_w/(\Sigma n_i - rc)$	
Total	$S_t = \Sigma\Sigma\Sigma (Y_{ijk} - Y_{\cdots})^2$	$\Sigma n_i - 1$		

Computer Program for Allocation of Costs in Environmental Amenities

```
FORTRAN IV G LEVEL  21              MAIN              DATE = 73269        17/26/10

            C  EJC FORMULATION OF AMENITIES ****
            C  **** FINAL VERSION   MARCH 1972 ****
            C  THIS PROGRAM CAN HANDLE UP TO 50 AMENITIES IN A TOTAL OF ARB. STATIONS
            C  WITH 11 LEVELS ALLOWED FOR EACH AMENITY....REVISIONS MAY BE MADE
            C  BY ADJUSTING DIMENSIONS HEREIN
   0001        INTEGER AMEN(50),MLVL(50),STA(50),INDEX(11)
   0002        DATA INDEX/11,10,9,8,7,6,5,4,3,2,1/
   0003        REAL R(50),STAWGT(50),D(50,11),U(50,11)
   0004        INTEGER ORIGLV(50)
   0005        SUM = C.C
   0006        ISUM = 0
            C  THE FOLLOWING DEFINITIONS EXIST
            C     AMEN(I)     AMENITY NUMBER
            C     STA(I)      STATION NUMBER OF AMENITY I
            C     MLVL(I)     INITIAL(ORIGINAL) LEVEL OF AMENITY I
            C                 NOTE...LEVEL 1 IS COMFORT
            C     R(I)        USER WEIGHT(RATING) FOR AMENITY I
            C     D(I,J)      CCST OF GOING FROM LEVEL J(PRESENT) TO NEXT BEST LEVEL
            C                 NOTE...D(I,1) NOT SPECIFIED SINCE #1 IS COMFORT
            C     STAWGT(I)   WEIGHT OF STATION HOUSING AMENITY I...STATION ADT..MOSTLY
   0007        COMMON/BLK1/AMEN,MLVL,STAWGT,R,D,STA
   0008        DO 30 I=1,50
   0009        DO 30 J = 1,11
   0010     30 D(I,J) = 0.0
   0011        CALL INPCT(N)
   0012        DO 40 I = 1,N
   0013     40 ORIGLV(I) = MLVL(I)
            C  INPUT COMPLETE...NOW CHECK
   0014        WRITE(6,90) INDEX
   0015     90 FORMAT('1',T11,'LISTING OF COSTS...AMENITIES VERTICAL...LEVELS HOR
              *IZCNTAL'/    T21,11I10//)
   0016        DO 100 I=1,N
   0017        WRITE(6,55) AMEN(I),(D(I,12-J),J=1,10)
   0018     95 FORMAT( 'O',T15,I5,T26,10F10.0)
   0019    100 CONTINUE
   0020        DO 120 I=1,N
   0021        KA = MLVL(I)
   0022        IF(D(I,KA).EQ.0.0.AND.MLVL(KA).NE.1) WRITE(6,110) I,KA
   0023    110 FORMAT('C',T21,'AMENITY',I4,'  HAS ILLEGAL STARTING LEVEL',I4)
   0024    120 CONTINUE
   0025        DO 200 I=1,N
   0026        NP =      MLVL(I)
   0027        IF(NP.EQ.1) GO TO 200
   0028        DO 130 J = 2,NP
   0029    130 U(I,J) =  (R(I)/D(I,J))*STAWGT(I)*FLOAT(J-1)
            C  NO D WITHIN  RANGE SHOULD BE ZERO
   0030    200 CONTINUE
   0031        WRITE(6,210)
   0032    210 FORMAT('1',T6,'TRANSITION RECORD',T26,'AMENITY',T34,'FROM LEVEL',
              1T46,'TO LEVEL',T56,'WEIGHT',T66,'COST',T76,'CUMULATIVE COST'///)
   0033        DO 220 I=1,N
   0034    220 ISUM = ISUM + MLVL(I)
   0035        DO 400 K = 1,50000
   0036                            IF(ISUM.EQ.N) GO TO  500
   0037        DUM =       0.0
   0038        DO 300 I=1,N
   0039        NP= MLVL(I)
   0040        IF(NP.EQ.1) GO TO 300
   0041        IF(U(I,NP).LT.DUM) GO TO 300
   0042        DUM = U(I,NP)
   0043        IDUM = I
   0044    300 CONTINUE
   0045        ISUM  = ISUM - 1
   0046        NP = MLVL(IDUM)
   0047        MLVL(IDUM) = MLVL(IDUM) - 1
   0048        SUM = SUM + D(IDUM,NP)
   0049        WRITE (6,320) AMEN(IDUM),NP,MLVL(IDUM),U(IDUM,NP),D(IDUM,NP),SUM
   0050    320 FORMAT(' ',T20,3I10,  E10.2,2F10.0)
   0051    400 CONTINUE
```

Allocation Program (cont.)

```
0052          500 CONTINUE
          C
          C   THIS IS NOW ORIGINAL APPROACH FOR COMPARISON
          C   RDBSTR  IS R  DOUBLE STAR
0053              REAL RDBSTR(50),X(50),NORRDS(50),COST(50),Y(50)
0054              INTEGER LEVELS(50)
0055              NZERO = 0
0056              DO 700 I = 1,N
0057              K = ORIGLV(I)
0058              IF(K.GT.1)  GO TO 610
0059              NZERO = NZERO + 1
0060              S = 1.0
0061              GO TO 650
0062          610 CONTINUE
0063          620 S = 0.0
0064              DO 640 J = 2,K
0065          640 S = S + D(I,J)
0066              S = S/FLOAT(K-1)
          C   S  IS NOW AVG COST
0067          650 CONTINUE
0068              RDBSTR(I) =(R(I)/S)*FLOAT(K-1)
0069          700 CONTINUE
0070              DEN = 0.0
0071              DO 710  I = 1, N
0072          710 DEN = DEN + RDBSTR(I)
0073              DEN  = DEN/FLOAT(N-NZERO)
0074              DO 720  I = 1,N
0075          720 NORRDS(I) = RDBSTR(I)/DEN
          C
          C   NORRDS IS NORMALIZED R DOUBLE STAR... NORMALIZED BY SUM
          C   OF ALL R DOUBLE STAR
          C
0076              MSTEP = 80
          C
          C   CAN CHANGE MSTEP AS DESIRED
          C
0077              DO 900 JE = 100,200
0078              WRITE(6,730) JE
0079          730 FORMAT('1',T16,'THIS IS ORIGINAL APPROACH WITH A FACTOR OF',I3///)
0080              WRITE(6,740) JE
0081          740 FORMAT(' ',T21,'AMENITY',T31,I2,'*RDBSTR',T46,'LEVELS MOVED',T61,
             1'COST'/)
0082              SUM = 0.0
0083              DO  790 I = 1,N
0084              X(I) = FLOAT(JE)*NORRDS(I) + 0.5
0085              LEVELS(I) = IFIX(X(I))
0086              KM = ORIGLV(I) - 1
0087              IF(LEVELS(I).GT.KM) LEVELS(I) = KM
0088              KEND = ORIGLV(I)
0089              KSTART = ORIGLV(I) - LEVELS(I) + 1
0090              IF (KSTART.GT.KEND) GO TO 760
0091              S = 0.0
0092              DO 750  K = KSTART,KEND
0093          750 S =  S + D(I,K)
0094              GO TO 770
0095          760 S=0
0096          770 CONTINUE
0097              SUM  = SUM + S
0098              Y(I) = FLOAT(JE)*RDBSTR(I)
0099              COST(I) = S
0100          790 CONTINUE
0101              DO 820 I = 1,N
0102              WRITE(6,800) AMEN(I),Y(I),LEVELS(I),COST(I)
0103          800 FORMAT(' ',T16,I10,T26,E10.2,T46,I5,T56,F10.0)
0104          820 CONTINUE
0105              WRITE(6,830) SUM
0106          830 FORMAT('0',T56,'***********'/T51,'SUM =',T56,F10.0)
0107          900 CONTINUE
0108              WRITE(6,600)
0109          600 FORMAT('0',T51,'FINISHED...EJC ')
0110              STOP
0111              END
```

Allocation Program (cont.)

```
0001            SUBROUTINE INPUT(N)
0002            REAL R(50),STAWGT(50), D(50,11)
0003            INTEGER AMEN(50),MLVL(50),S(10),STA(50)
0004            COMMON/BLK1/AMEN,MLVL,STAWGT,R,D,STA
        C
        C THERE MAY BE
        C      NSTA      STATIONS
        C      NAMEN     AMENITIES IN EACH STATION (SAME IN EACH)
        C AS LONG AS  NSTA*NAMEN  DOES NOT EXCEED 50...UNLESS DIMENSIONS REVISED
0005            READ(5,100) NSTA,NAMEN
0006    100 FORMAT(8X,I2,8X,I2)
0007            REAL UNIT(20,11)
        C  UNIT COSTS NOW TO BE READ IN
        C  NOTE NAMEN RESTRICTED TO 20 OR  LESS
0008            DO  200  I  = 1,NAMEN
0009            READ(5,120)    (UNIT(I,12-J),J=1,10)
0010    120 FORMAT(6X,F9.0,10X,F10.0,10X,F10.0,10X,F10.0)
0011    200 CONTINUE
        C  STATION AMENITIES  NOW TO BE READ WITH BASIC DATA
        C
0012            N = NSTA*NAMEN
0013            READ(5,205) STUP
0014    205 FORMAT(A4)
0015            DO 300 J=1,N
0016            READ(5,210)  NA,NB,XA,NC,XB
0017    210 FORMAT(4X,I2,7X,I2,F9.0,12X,I2,F11.0)
0018            I = (NA-1)*NAMEN+ NB
0019            AMEN(I) = I
0020            R(I) = XA
0021            MLVL(I) = NC
0022            STAWGT(I) = XB
0023            STA(I) = NA
0024    300 CONTINUE
0025            READ(5,310) NSPEC
0026    310 FORMAT(25X,I5)
        C
        C  NSPEC  INDICATES NUMBER OF ROUTE AMENITIES...AMENITIES SUCH AS TRAIN
        C  SERVICE REALIZED AT SEVERAL  STATIONS OR NOT AT ALL
0027            IF(NSPEC.EQ.0) GO TO 455
0028            DO 450  J = 1,NSPEC
0029            READ(5,320) NA,S
0030    320 FORMAT(8X,I2,10X,10I5)
0031            DO 340 KA = 1,10
0032            K = KA - 1
0033            IF(S(KA).EQ.0) GO TO 350
0034    340 CONTINUE
0035            K=10
0036    350 CONTINUE
0037            KA = (S(1)-1)*NAMEN+ NA
0038            DO 360  KB = 2,K
0039            KC =(S(KB) - 1)* NAMEN + NA
0040            STAWGT(KA) = STAWGT(KA) + STAWGT(KC)
0041            STAWGT(KC) = 0.0
0042            MLVL(KC) = 1
0043    360 CONTINUE
        C
        C  NOTE THAT THIS  AMEN  GIVEN TO ONE STATION FOR BOOKKEEPING
        C  BUT GIVEN WEIGHT FROM ALL  STATIONS IT AFFECTS
        C
0044    450 CONTINUE
        C
        C   NOW READ BASIC DIMENSIONS FOR EACH STATION
        C THE FOLLOWING BASIC DIMENSIONS ARE NEEDED FOR EACH STATION
        C       X(1)    SQ FT FLOOR SPACE
        C       X(2)    FT  RISE
        C       X(3)    CUBIC FT VOLUME
        C       X(4)    SQ FT CEILING
        C       X(5)    SQ FT  WALL SPACE
        C       X(6)    MILES OF RUN FOR TRAIN ROUTE
        C       X(7)    PEAK HOUR VOLUME(GREATER VOLUME APPLIC. TO ESCALATORS
        C       X(8)    FT LENGTH
        C       X(9)    NUM TRACKS
        C THESE SHALL BE ENTERED INTO AN ARRAY  X(10,9) WHERE UP TO 10 STATIONS ARE OK
0045            REAL X(10,9)
0046    455 CONTINUE
0047            READ(5,205) STVP
0048            READ(5,205) STVP
0049            DO 500 J = 1,NSTA
0050            READ(5,460)   (X(J,K),K=1,9)
0051    460 FORMAT(10X,7F10.0)
```

Allocation Program (cont.)

```
0052          500 CONTINUE
        C
        C     SPECIAL CARE MUST BE TAKEN THAT THE UNITS IN
        C     THE MATERIAL TO FOLLOW ARE CONSISTENT WITH INTENDED UNITS
        C
0053          DO 1000 J =1,NSTA
0054          I = (J-1)*NAMEN + 1
        C     *                                                        *  NOTE      *
        C     *     THE FOLLOWING PART OF THE PROGRAM IS SPECIFIC TO THE *  BASIC     *
        C     *     CASE STRUCTURE...OK FOR EJC'S 11 AMENITIES IN GIVEN ORDER * DISCRETE *
        C     *                                                        *  UNITS     *
0055          IA =  (X(J,1)/20000.0) + 0.9
0056          IF(IA.EQ.0) IA = 1
0057          DO 600 K = 2, 6
0058      600 D(I,K) = IA*UNIT(1,K)
0059          IA = (X(J,7)/6000.0) + 0.6                                      6000
0060          IF(IA.EQ.0) IA = 1
0061          DO 610 K = 2,8
0062      610 D(I+1,K) = IA*UNIT(2,K)
0063          IC = (X(J,3)/1.0) + 1.0                                           1
0064          DO 620 K = 2,10
0065      620 D(I+2,K) = IC*UNIT(3,K)
0066          IA = (X(J,1)/1.0) + 1.0                                           1
0067          IB = (X(J,4)/1.0) + 1.0                                           1
0068          IC = (X(J,5)/1.0) + 1.0                                           1
0069          ID = (X(J,1)/20000.0) + 1.0                                   20000

0070          IF(ID.EQ.0) ID = 1
0071          DO 630 K = 6,8
0072      630 D(I+3,K) =  IB*UNIT(4,K)
0073          D(I+3,5) =   ID*UNIT(4,5)
0074          D(I+3,4) =   IA*UNIT(4,4)
0075          D(I+3,3) =   IC*UNIT(4,3)
0076          D(I+3,2) =   IB*UNIT(4,2)
0077          IA = (X(J,6)/1.0) + 0.5                                           1
0078          DO 640 K = 2,5
0079          D(I+4,K) = IA*UNIT(5,K)
0080      640 D(I+5,K) = IA*UNIT(6,K)
0081          IA = (X(J,8)/1.0)                                                 1
0082          IB = (X(J,9)/1.0)                                                 1
0083          IC = (X(J,4)+X(J,5))/1.0                                      1 AND 1
0084          D(I+6,6) =  IA*IB*UNIT(7,6)
0085          D(I+6,5) =     IB*UNIT(7,5)
0086          D(I+6,4) =  IA*IB*UNIT(7,4)
0087          D(I+6,3) =     IC*UNIT(7,3)
0088          D(I+6,2) =  IA*IB*UNIT(7,2)
0089          IA =  X(J,1)/1.0                                                  1
0090          DO 660 K = 2,5
0091      660 D(I+7,K) = IA*UNIT(8,K)
0092          IA = (X(J,1)/20000.0) + 0.4                                   20000
0093          IF(IA.EQ.0) IA = 1
0094          DO 670 K = 2,6
0095      670 D(I+8,K) = IA*UNIT(9,K)
0096          IA =  X(J,3)/1.0                                                  1
0097          DO 680 K= 2,7
0098      680 D(I+9,K) = IA*UNIT(10,K)
0099          IA = (X(J,1)/20000.0) + 0.4                                   20000
0100          IF(IA.EQ.0) IA = 1
0101          DO 690 K= 2,7
0102      690 D(I+10,K) = IA*UNIT(11,K)
        C     *                                              *            *
        C     *     THIS ENDS THE SPECIFIC PART OF           *            *
        C     *     THIS RUN                                 *            *
        C                                                    *            *
0103     1000 CONTINUE
        C THE FOLLOWING OVERLOAD FIGURES WERE USED
        C     AMEN 1  (CLEANING)              10  PER CENT (SQ FT)
        C          2  (ESCALATORS)            40  PER CENT (PERSONS)
        C          4  (REDECORATION)          60  PER CENT (FURNITURE)
        C          5  (TRAINS)                50  PER CENT (MILES)
        C          6  (TRAINS)                50  PER CENT (MILES)
        C  IN 5 AND 6, THIS IS JUST ROUNDING TO THE NEAREST MILE
        C          9  (POLICE)                60  PER CENT (SQ FT)
        C          11 (WASHROOMS)             60  PER CENT (SQ FT)
        C  FOR EXAMPLE, THERE MUST BE A 40 PER CENT OVERLOAD ON AN EXISTING
        C  ESCALATOR(MORE PROPERLY,40 PER CENT OR MORE THAT THE NEXT ESCALATOR
        C  WOULD USE) BEFORE IT IS CONSIDERED...A MINIMUM OF 1 IS ALWAYS CONSIDERED
        C
        C
0104          RETURN
0105          END
```

Notes

Notes

Introduction

1. *Tomorrow's Transportation*, U.S. Department of Housing and Urban Development, Washington, D.C., 1968.
2. "New Concepts in Urban Transportation Systems," in *The Journal of the Franklin Institute*, Vol. 286, No. 5, Nov. 1968.
3. Ibid.
4. A.R. Sloan and J.W. Blatteau, *Reestablishing the Link*, Southeastern Pennsylvania Transportation Authority, January 1970.
5. Ibid.
6. R. Evans, "Sick Transit," in *Humble Way*, Vol. 9, 1970.
7. Ibid.
8. M.T. Shaffer, "Attitude Techniques in Action," in *Highway Research Record* No. 305, 1970.
9. F. Herzberg, et al., *The Motivation to Work*, John Wiley & Sons, New York, 1959.
10. M. Wachs, "Basic Approaches to the Measurement of Community Values," in *Highway Research Record* No. 305, 1970.

Chapter 1
Allocation Techniques and
"Community Values"

1. J.L. Sorenson, "Identification of Social Costs & Benefits in Urban Transportation," in *Systems Analysis of Urban Transportation*, Vol. 3: Network Flow Analyses, General Research Corp., January 1968, Santa Barbara, California, January 1968.
2. H. Mohring, "Urban Highway Investments," in R. Dorfman, ed., *Measuring Benefits of Government Investments*, The Brookings Institute, 1964.
3. M. Wachs, "Basic Approaches to the Measurement of Community Values," in *Highway Research Record* No. 305, 1970.
4. Sorenson, "Social Costs & Benefits in Urban Transportation."
5. J.D. Crumlish, "Notes on the State of the Art of Benefit-Cost Analysis as Related to Transportation Systems," U.S. Dept. of Commerce, Bureau of Standards, *N.B.S. Technical Note 294*, 1966.
6. C.W. Churchman, R.L. Ackoff, E.L. Arnoff, *Introduction to Operations Research*, John Wiley & Sons, Inc., New York, 1957.
7. P.C. Fishburn, "Utility Theory," in *Management Science*, Vol. 14, No. 5, January 1968.
8. E.W. Adams, "Elements of a Theory of Inexact Measurements," in *Philosophy of Science*, Vol. 32, 1965.

9. Wachs, "Measurement of Community Values."

10. O.H. Coolidge and G.C. Reier, "An Appraisal of Received Telephone Speech Volume," in *Bell System Technical Journal*, Vol. 38, May 1959.

11. *Qualitative Aspects of Urban Personal Travel Demand*, Abt Associates, Inc., August 1968.

12. F.M. Bass, et al., "Market Segmentation: Group Versus Individual Behavior," in *Journal of Marketing Research*, August 1968.

13. R.K. McMillan and H. Assael, "National Survey of Transportation Attitudes & Behavior," HRB, Washington, D.C., 1968.

14. W. Jessiman, et al., "A Rational Decision-Making Technique for Transportation Planning," in *Highway Research Record 180*, 1967.

15. E.N. Dodson, "Cost-Effectiveness in Urban Transportation," in *Operations Research*, May-June 1969, Operations Research Society of America.

16. Ibid.

17. *Traffic Signal System Study*, Department of Transit & Traffic, City of Baltimore, Maryland, Peat, Marwick, Livingston & Co., February 1969.

18. Churchman, et al., *Operations Research.*

19. *Traffic Signal System Study.*

20. E.N. Dodson, "Cost-Benefit Scales for Urban Transportation," in *System Analysis of Urban Transportation*, Vol. 3: Network Flow Analyses, General Research Corp. January 1968, Santa Barbara, California, August 1967.

21. Sorenson, "Social Costs and Benefits in Urban Transportation."

22. G. Hadley, *Non-Linear and Dynamic Programming*, Addison Wesley, Reading, Massachusetts, 1964.

Chapter 2
Assessing "Community Values"

1. R.K. McMillan and H. Assael, "National Survey of Transportation Attitudes & Behavior," HRB, Washington, D.C., 1968.

2. T.E. Lisco, "Value of Commuters Travel Time—A Study in Urban Transportation," in H.R. Record No. 245, 1968.

3. *National Survey of Transportation Attitudes & Behavior, Phase I*, NCHRP Report 49, HRB, Washington, D.C., 1968; *Phase II*, NCHRP Report 82, HRB, Washington, D.C., 1969.

4. G.A. Brunner, et al., "User Determined Attributes of Ideal Transportation Systems: An Empirical Study," University of Maryland, College Park, Maryland, June 1966 (PB 173 730).

5. A.M. Sommers and F.F. Leimkuhler, "A Nondemographic Factor V/STOL Prediction Model," in *ORSA Bulletin*, Vol. 16, Supplement 2, Fall 1968.

6. S.J. Hille, et al., *Studying Transportation Systems from the Consumer Viewpoint: Some Recommendations*, Maryland University, September 1967 (PB 176 484).

7. P.M. Williams, "Low Fares and the Urban Transport Problem," in *Urban Studies*, May 1968.

8. R.W. Smith, *A Pilot Study of Relationships Between Socio-Economic Factors, User Attitudes & Preferences & Urban Transportation System Attributes,* Damas & Smith Ltd., Toronto, Canada, April 1969.

9. O. Perilla, "Findings of a Survey on Residence & Travel Selections by Households—Part IV: Some Factors in Choice of Mode Combinations for Journey to Work, Report 70-4," PONYA Engineering Dept. Res. & Dev. Div. (unpublished), March 1970.

10. Final Report, *Project DATA*, Vol. 3, Appendixes, Case Western Reserve University, et al., Cleveland, Ohio, May 1969.

11. A.N. Sommers, "The Transportation Analyst and the Social Environment," in *High Speed Ground Transportation Journal*, Vol. 3, No. 2, May 1969.

12. C.E. Osgood, et al., *The Measurement of Meaning*, University of Illinois Press, Urbana, Illinois, 1957.

13. T.F. Paine, et al., *Consumer Conceived Attributes of Transportation: An Attitude Study*, University of Maryland, College Park, Maryland, 1967 (PB 176 485).

14. C. Scott, "Research on Mail Surveys," in *Journal of the Royal Statistical Society*, Series A, 124, 1961.

Chapter 3
Some Human Environmental
Factors

1. K.M. Solomon, R.J. Solomon, and J.S. Silien, *Passenger Psychological Dynamics*, Journal of Urban Transportation Corp. and ASCE, New York, 1968.

2. J.K. Sheehan, *A Discussion of Transit Car Features*, Operations Research Inc., for National Capital Transportation Agency, June 1964.

3. Solomon, et al., *Passenger Psychological Dynamics.*

4. Ibid.

5. J.J. Fruin, "Environmental Factors in Passenger Terminal Design," Meeting Preprint 1280, ASCE Annual & National Environmental Engineering Meeting, New York, N.Y., October 19-22, 1970.

6. "Cost Information from the New York City Transit Authority" (Unpublished), July 9, 1971.

7. "Less Comfort Stations," in *Long Island Press*, May 24, 1971.

8. "Cost Information from the NYC Transit Authority."

9. Final Report, Project DATA Vol. 3, Appendixes, Case Western Reserve University, et al., Cleveland, Ohio, May 1969.

10. L.M. Kashin, "Effects of Small Concentrations of Carbon Disulfide on Certain Functions & Organs of Animals," in *Vestnik* of the U.S.S.R. Academy of Medical Sciences, Vol. XXI, No. 8, 1966.

11. "TA Rates Its Air Above Ground," in *The New York Post*, December 13, 1971.

12. *Tomorrow's Transportation*, U.S. Dept. of Housing and Urban Development, Washington, D.C., 1968.

13. Ibid.

14. Final Report, Project DATA.

15. J.J. Fruin, "Environmental Factors in Passenger Terminal Design," Meeting Preprint 1280, ASCE Annual & National Environmental Engineering Meeting, New York, N.Y., October 19-22, 1970.

16. "Subways Need Not Be Sewers," in *The Architectural Forum*, January-February 1968.

17. "Cost Information from the NYC Transit Authority."

18. "Staff Supplementary Report to the Program for Mass Transportation of the Massachusetts Bay Transportation Authority" (unpublished), August 1966.

19. Fruin, "Passenger Terminal Design."

20. Final Report, Project DATA.

21. "Ideal Work Conditions," in the *New York Post*, October 22, 1970.

22. K.A. Provins and C.R. Bell, "Effects of Heat Stress on the Performance of Two Tasks Running Concurrently," in *Journal of Experimental Psychology*, Vol. 85, No. 1, 1970.

23. G. Kh. Shakhbazyan and F. M. Shleyfman, "Adaptation of the Body to Temperature Fluctuations," in *Vestnik* of the U.S.S.R. Academy of Medical Sciences, Vol. XXI, No. 8, 1966.

24. C.H. Wyndham, et al., "Changes in Central Circulation & Body Fluid Spaces During Acclimatization to Heat," in *Journal of Applied Physiology*, Vol. 25, No. 5, November 1968.

25. J.F. Wing, "Upper Thermal Tolerance Limits for Unimpaired Mental Performance," in *Aerospace Medicine*, October 1965.

26. R.H. Fox, et al., "Comparison of Thermoregulatory Function in Men & Women," in *Journal of Applied Physiology*, Vol. 26, No. 4, April 1969.

27. *Tomorrow's Transportation.*

28. L.L. Beranek and L.N. Miller, "The Anatomy of Noise," in *Machine Design*, September 14, 1967.

29. V. Salmon, "Noise in Mass-Transit Systems," in *Stanford Research Institute Journal* No. 16, September 1967.

30. E.W. Davis, *Comparison of Noise & Vibration Levels in Rapid Transit Vehicle Systems*, Operations Research, Inc., for National Capital Transportation Agency, April 1964.

31. Salmon, "Noise in Mass-Transit Systems."

32. Ibid.

33. Davis, *Noise & Vibration.*

34. Salmon, "Noise in Mass-Transit Systems."

35. J.D. Dougherty, "Community Noise & Hearing Loss," in *New England Journal of Medicine*, October 6, 1966.

36. J.H. Winchester, "Is Noise Driving You Crazy?" in *Science Digest*, August 1964.

37. "That Noise You Hear May Be Pollution: Scientists Fighting Noise Pollution," in *Business Week*, April 22, 1967.

38. M. Brower, "Noise Pollution: A Growing Menace," in *Saturday Review*, May 27, 1967.

39. C.M. Harris, "Noise," in *Environmental Science & Technology*, April 1967.

40. H.M. David, "Infrasound Tests Human Tolerance," in *Missiles & Rockets*, October 11, 1965.

41. R.W. Shoenberger and C.S. Harris, "Human Performance as a Function of Changes in Acoustic Noise Levels," in *Journal of Engineering Psychology*, Vol. 4, No. 4, 1965.

42. A.A. Arkad'yevskiy, "Hygienic Standards for Constant Noise in Industry," in *Gigiyena i Sanitarya* No. 7, Moscow, July 1964.

43. David, "Infrasound Tests Human Tolerance."

44. C. Morgan et al., *Human Engineering Guide to Equipment Design*, McGraw-Hill Book Company, New York, 1963.

45. "Anti-Noise Plan Takes Shape," in *Long Island Press*, July 4, 1971.

46. "All Quiet in New Jersey," editorial in *The New York Times*, Friday, January 28, 1972.

47. "Moscow Hears Clamor for Earplugs," in *The New York Times*, Friday, January 28, 1972.

48. "Cost Information from the NYC Transit Authority."

49. Ibid.

50. Solomon, et al., *Passenger Psychological Dynamics.*

51. Salmon, "Noise in Mass-Transit Systems."

52. J.I. Soliman, "A Scale for the Degrees of Vibration Perceptibility & Annoyance," in *Ergonomics*, Vol. 11, No. 2, 1968.

53. W.E. Woodson and D.W. Conover, *Human Engineering Guide for Equipment Designers* (2nd ed.), University of California Press, Berkeley, 1964, pp. 2-227.

54. Solomon, et al., *Passenger Psychological Dynamics.*

55. Woodson and Conover, *Human Engineering Guide for Equipment Designers.*

56. "Cost Information from the NYC Transit Authority."

57. A.R. Sloan and J.W. Blatteau, *Reestablishing the Link*, Southeastern Pennsylvania Transportation Authority, January 1970.

58. *Tomorrow's Transportation.*

59. Final Report, Project DATA.

60. Solomon, et al., *Passenger Psychological Dynamics.*

61. Final Report, Project DATA.

62. H. Megel, "The Effect of Heat, Vibration & the Combination of Heat & Vibration Upon Tolerance Levels of Rats," in *Boeing Document D2-9766*, 1961.

63. R.D. Dean and C.L. McGothlen, "Effects of Combined Heat & Noise on Human Performance, Psychology, & Subjective Estimates of Comfort & Per-

formance," in *Proceedings of the Institute of Environmental Sciences*, Chicago, April 21-23, 1965, Annual Technical Meeting.

64. W.L. Jenkins, "Somesthesis," Chapter 30, in *Handbook of Experimental Psychology*, S.S. Stevens (ed.), Wiley, New York, 1951.

65. J.P. Nafe and K.W. Wagoner, "The Experiences of Warmth, Cold & Heat," in *J. Psycol.*, 2, 1936.

66. Dean and McGothlen, "Effects of Combined Heat & Noise."

67. K.K. Ioseliani, "The Effect of Vibration & Noise on the Mental Faculty of Man Under Time Stress," in *Kosmicheskaya Biologiya i Meditsina*, Vol. 1, No. 2, 1967.

Chapter 5
Test Values: Patron Opinion

1. G.A. Brunner, et al., "User Determined Attributes of Ideal Transportation Systems: An Empirical Study," University of Maryland, College Park, Maryland, June 1966 (PB 173 730).

2. A.N. Sommers, "The Transportation Analyst and the Social Environment," in *High Speed Ground Transportation Journal*, Vol. 3, No. 2, May 1969.

3. C. Scott, "Research on Mail Surveys," in *Journal of the Royal Statistical Society*, Series A, 124, 1961.

4. E.G. Francel, "Mail-Administered Questionnaires: A Success Story," in *Journal of Marketing Research*, February 1966.

5. M. Friedman, "The Use of Ranks to Avoid the Assumption of Normality Implicit in the Analysis of Variance," in *Journal of the American Statistical Association*, No. 32, 1937.

6. M.G. Kendall, *Rank Correlation Methods*, Hafner, New York, 1955.

7. R.A. Fisher, *Statistical Methods for Research Workers*, Hafner, New York, 1950.

8. R. Langley, *Practical Statistics*, Dover, New York, 1970.

9. E.J. Cantilli, A.A. Engelberg, and L.J. Pignataro, "Introducing Public Opinion into Resource-Allocation for Public Transportation," unpublished monograph, Department of Transportation Planning & Engineering, PIB, 1971.

Chapter 6
Test Values: Acceptable
Comfort Levels

1. "Cost Information from the New York City Transit Authority" (unpublished), July 9, 1971.

2. W. Lassow, E.L. Lustenader, and K. Schoch, *A Thermal Model for the Evaluation of Subway Ventilation and Air Conditioning*, 1971, ASCE-ASME

National Transportation Engineering Meeting, Seattle, Washington, July 26-30, 1971.

3. J.H. Winchester, "Is Noise Driving You Crazy?" in *Science Digest*, August 1964.

4. D.C. Hay, (untitled), in *Today's Health*, January 1972.

5. J.J. Fruin, *Pedestrian Planning and Design*, MAUDEP Press, New York, N.Y., 1971.

Chapter 7
Test Values: Improvements Cost

1. "Cost Information from the New York City Transit Authority" (unpublished), July 9, 1971.

2. *Building Construction Cost Data*, Means, Duxbury, Massachusetts, 1970.

3. J.J. Fruin, "Environmental Factors in Passenger Terminal Design," Meeting Preprint 1280, ASCE Annual & National Environmental Engineering Meeting, New York, N.Y., October 19-22, 1970.

4. "Cost Information from the NYC Transit Authority."

5. *Building Construction Cost Data.*

6. "Cost Information from the NYC Transit Authority."

7. Ibid.

8. Fruin, "Environmental Factors in Passenger Terminal Design."

9. Ibid.

10. "Cost Information from the NYC Transit Authority."

11. Ibid.

12. *Building Construction Cost Data.*

13. "Cost Information from the NYC Transit Authority."

Index

About the Author

Edmund J. Cantilli joined the faculty of the Polytechnic Institute of Brooklyn's (now the Polytechnic Institute of New York) newly formed Department of Transportation Planning and Engineering in 1969 after many years as a practicing planner and engineer with the Port Authority of New York-New Jersey. He has directed and participated in research projects in many aspects of transportation, including environmental effects, transportation for the disadvantaged, and various traffic-congestion and safety problems. Dr. Cantilli is also active as a professional consultant, is an active member of planning and engineering professional societies, and is the author and/or editor of numerous articles and books in the various subjects of his interest.